"Willie is the Earth and ecology's best friend. Read this brilliant treatise for how to get off petrochemicals and into ecologically and economically sustainable biodiesel."

—Mark Victor Hansen, coauthor of *The New York Times* best-selling Chicken Soup for the Soul series

"*On the Clean Road Again* provides a surprisingly insightful mix of thought-provoking information and classic Willie wit. It is a fast, entertaining read that makes you think about some of the big issues, such as energy, agriculture, and conservation, that will help shape the way we will fuel our economy and feed our families in the future."

—Joe Jobe, CEO, National Biodiesel Board

"Willie Nelson takes a serious subject and makes the information entertaining—sometimes laugh-out-loud funny. This is a must-read for folks who care about our addiction to oil but prefer their education 'light.' He informs us, yet he makes it as much fun as kickin' up our heels in a Texas two-step!"

—Carol Sue Tombari, former director of the Texas State Energy Conservation Office

Speaker's Corner Books

is a provocative new series designed to stimulate, educate, and foster discussion on significant public policy topics. Written by experts in a variety of fields, these brief and engaging books should be read by anyone interested in the trends and issues that shape our society.

Other related titles

in the Speaker's Corner series

The Enduring Wilderness:
Protecting Our Natural Heritage through the Wilderness Act
  Doug Scott

Ethics for a Finite World:
An Essay Concerning a Sustainable Future
  Herschel Elliott

Power of the People:
America's New Electricity Choices
  Carol Sue Tombari

Stop Global Warming:
The Solution Is You!
  Laurie David

More thought-provoking titles

in the Speaker's Corner series

Brave New World of Health Care
  Richard D. Lamm

Condition Critical:
A New Moral Vision for Health Care
  Richard D. Lamm and Robert H. Blank

God and Caesar in America:
An Essay on Religion and Politics
  Gary Hart

For more information, visit our Web site,
  www.fulcrumbooks.com

On the _∧Clean Road Again

Biodiesel and the Future of the Family Farm

On the ^Clean Road Again

Biodiesel and the Future of the Family Farm

Willie Nelson

 Fulcrum Publishing

Golden, Colorado

Library of Congress Cataloging-in-Publication Data
Nelson, Willie, 1933-
    On the clean road again: biodiesel and the future of the family farm / by Willie Nelson.
        p. cm. -- (Speakers' corner books)
    ISBN 1-55591-624-4 (pbk.)
    1. Biodiesel fuels--United States. 2. Vegetable oils as fuel--United States. I. Title.
    TP359.B46N45 2007
    662'.88--dc22

                                                2007014376

Printed in Canada by Friesens Corporation
0 9 8 7 6 5 4 3 2 1

Design: Jack Lenzo
Editorial: Sam Scinta, Haley Berry, Faith Marcovecchio
Cover Image: David Zettner

Fulcrum Publishing
4690 Table Mountain Drive, Suite 100
Golden, Colorado 80403
800-992-2908 • 303-277-1623
www.fulcrumbooks.com

Contents

Foreword

It was with some amount of trepidation that I accepted the honor of writing this foreword to Willie Nelson's book *On the Clean Road Again*. Willie is a legend in so many ways: a world-famous musician, songwriter, and singer; a powerful voice for the American farmer; and now a leader and spokesperson helping create the new U.S. biodiesel industry. I have made the choice to devote my life to the effort of developing smarter, cleaner renewable fuels, so having this once-in-a-lifetime opportunity to introduce a groundbreaking book on biodiesel written by my friend Willie Nelson is both an honor and a great responsibility.

In 200 years, when people look back to the beginning of the biodiesel industry, they will see a growth curve that began in 1992 and dramatically accelerated in 2004, when Willie Nelson became involved after his wife, Annie Nelson, introduced him to biodiesel. Willie has worked tirelessly for most of his life to assist the American farmer, and now, through biodiesel, Willie is becoming a pretty good farmer himself. Every week, as he travels our country talking with people and playing his music, Willie plants the seeds of knowledge about biodiesel as a better fuel alternative to petroleum. To highlight his personal commitment, he leads by example: his tour bus runs on biodiesel, and so do his family's vehicles. Those priceless seeds of awareness and change planted by Willie each day will grow and bear fruit for generations to come, and the benefits will be endless.

Anyone who has spent time with Willie knows that family is the most important part of his life. What makes him different in that respect is that Willie considers everyone who works hard to make things better for the environment—the farmer, the trucker, the teacher, the average American—part of his extended family. He is extremely generous with his time and his support for the causes he believes will make the world a better place.

You will enjoy this book. It will help you learn, make you think, and hopefully start you traveling on the clean road of biodiesel and renewable fuel. We can't leave it all up to Willie; we each have to make the decision to change and then take action to make things better for future generations. Biodiesel is helping farm communities grow again. Truckers plan their fueling patterns to ensure they get biodiesel-blended fuel. Consumers are buying diesel-powered cars to improve mileage and to burn cleaner biodiesel fuels. Teachers are including biodiesel in their lesson plans. What will you do?

Let's get to work. Go biodiesel!

—Jason Hoar
president, AgriFuels, LLC

Foreword

When I was asked to contribute to this great project, I was certainly happy to do so, though I was a little concerned that my mind may have been cluttered with too many years of academia to keep up with Willie's razor-sharp wit. So hopefully Willie will sprinkle some of his magic dust on this chapter to make it enjoyably digestible to the good reader.

An extended group of us has been on this biofuels ride, for better or worse, since its humble beginnings. Many of us got into this budding industry driven by a simple belief that America can do better, as a nation and as citizens. We discovered that with biofuels we can prosper without pollution and without giving more American blood to the Middle East for oil. We share a simple belief that we, as individuals working together, really can change the world … one gallon at a time.

As the concept of renewable, American-made fuel gained steam and spirit, we came from the farm, from industry, from academia; hell, we came from everywhere. But the important part is that we came and that there are more of us every day. Willie and Annie, whether they asked for it or not, have become the spiritual compass for this evolving eco-industry. They get the big picture and have the microphone, along with other ethical celebrities, to speak to the America we all know is still in this country. The America that, phony politics aside, values its roots and independence. Producing and using homegrown fuel is as patriotic as you can get, my friends, and that is the vision we are proposing. We are taking all motivated recruits for this journey of patriotic sustainability. Interested? Well, welcome aboard.

I won't pretend that this industry is made up entirely of eco-Americana saints, but the vision is there at the core of the movement, in the shared vision that we can, with the help of the American farmer, take our nation back from the talons of the petroleum lobby and the games of the Middle East. We can give folks a choice to fuel up with a cleaner-burning, American-made fuel, a choice to drive the American highway with all the pleasure and none of the guilt. We can build a business and industry that's ethical, sustainable, *and* profitable. Although you might think otherwise—with all the "mini-Trumps" running around wanting to profit at any cost—you *can* do well by doing good. The renewable-fuels industry holds that promise if it keeps its roots and spirit.

There will always be snakes in the grass who slither through an industry (and some are in it now), but if we stay focused on the bigger picture and remember why we got into this game, there's no doubt in my mind that we can make this thing happen; we can change the way fuel is made in this country.

There should be no illusion about the challenge we face in bringing farm-grown fuel to the American consumer. After all, we're talking about what the academics call a paradigm shift, a fancy term that means we have to fundamentally change the way people think about and operate within a given model.

One model is the status quo. It goes a little something like this: We suck "dinosaur juice" out of an Arab desert

10,000 miles from where it will be used. We send our sons and daughters, at cost of life and limb, to escort the black gold to our shores, where we all lap it up with an insatiable appetite. We have a national addiction to unsustainable consumption. Anybody ready for rehab? First step: admit there is a problem. That's the easy part, right?

Our petroleum addiction comes at a cost: a cost to our energy security, a cost to the air we breathe, a cost to the planet's climatic systems that we depend on, and, most of all, a cost to our children and the spirit that made this country great.

Americans innovate; that's what we do. It doesn't make a damn bit of sense that in the twenty-first century we are pumping dinosaur carbon out of the ground and into the sky in order to move from point A to point B, all at our kids' long-term expense. We are smarter than that, and if it weren't for a handful of powerful dealers in gray suits who profit from our nation's gluttonous addiction, we might have pulled out of this a long time ago.

But there is hope! And hope is happening. Let's be clear: biofuels are here and now and can make a real difference, but there is not just one silver bullet. We need a fundamental paradigm shift to get this monkey off our country's back. That shift starts with you and me, all of us, real Americans committed to taking their country back and changing the world, one gallon at a time.

—Jake Stewart
vice president of corporate development and R & D,
Biodiesel Industries

Introduction
I Can't Wait to Get on the Road Again

I'd like to help revive an old idea: the idea of the American farmer growing our fuel. Until recently, most folks had nearly forgotten about food-based fuel, but with the current oil shortages and high prices, approximately 130 million cars on the road in the United States, and 170,000 gas stations selling approximately 130 billion gallons of gas per year to fuel them, it seems to me that there's no time like the present to reach into the past.

Family farmers already produce the required energy for a healthy body; why not let them produce the energy for our rapidly escalating transportation needs too? I believe this growing trend toward alternative energy will reduce our dependency on foreign oil while simultaneously saving the American family farm.

My wife, Annie, first introduced me to the idea of burning vegetable oil for fuel. She wanted to buy a new diesel Volkswagen Jetta and intended to run it on something called biodiesel instead of conventional petroleum-based diesel gasoline. I had never even heard of biodiesel. She explained that biodiesel burns cleaner and safer and is better for the environment. I already knew that Europeans grew their own home-heating oil, but I never dreamed you could actually run a car on food.

Annie bought the diesel car, and she fills it with 100

percent biodiesel every time. It worked so well for her, I decided I needed a diesel car and bought a brand-new diesel Mercedes. The first thing I did was fill it up with 100 percent biodiesel. It's been three years now, and I haven't had one problem with it. A company in Maui called Pacific Biodiesel goes around the island and takes used cooking oil and grease from the grease traps in local restaurants, processes it, and turns it into a burnable, clean, safe alternative diesel fuel called biodiesel. So sometimes when you're driving behind a biodiesel-fueled car, the exhaust smells like piping hot donuts or french fries.

One hundred percent biodiesel is completely safe too. Annie and I pull up, fill up, and leave knowing we've made a difference. We've made a contribution to a cleaner environment, and we didn't have to go all the way to the Middle East to get biodiesel. It was right here in our own backyard.

Part I: The Past

The Black Mistress

When I began to research biodiesel and what it could mean for the family farmer, I discovered that the notion of our American farmers growing fuel for the nation isn't even new. We started using vegetable oil in big engines in the late 1800s, when the first diesel engine was introduced.

German inventor Rudolf Diesel presented the peanut oil–fueled Black Mistress to the world in 1893. Since then, diesel engines have become an everyday staple in the lives of billions of people around the world. They're in the farm equipment out in the cotton fields around my Texas hometown; there's one in my farming friend Morris Russell's old pickup; there are three in my buses, one in my nephew Freddie's boat, and thousands in the trains that run through the middle of Abbott. Do you know the most amazing thing about the diesel engine? It's now over 100 years old and it still runs on peanut oil.

According to historians, Rudolf Diesel was a pacifist and the thought of his wonderful humanitarian machine being used as a war weapon repulsed him. World War I had begun, and the Germans were putting the diesel engine in their U-boats. He voiced his opposition loudly, but was silenced forever by his mysterious death on September 30, 1913, after either being thrown overboard or committing suicide by jumping into the English Channel. He was fifty-five years old. Rudolf Diesel may be gone, but the children of his Black Mistress still live on.

About the time the diesel engine was gaining popularity, the president of the United States, Theodore Roosevelt, picked up on another German idea and encouraged our farmers to begin growing the United States' fuel. Germany was seeing tremendous success with growing rape, an inedible plant with very high oil content. The ingenious German people were burning rapeseed oil in their homes for light and heat, replacing the usual kerosene and whale oil.

President Roosevelt wanted to see the same success for American farmers. He spearheaded legislation lifting taxes on alcohol for industrial uses, which included the production of ethanol. Ethanol is made by fermenting grain, starchy vegetables such as corn or potatoes, or even sugary plants like cane or sugar beets. The fermented alcohol is then burned as fuel. In the spring, American farmers grew the corn, potatoes, or grain and then brewed their fall harvest in simple stills, transforming the sugary concoction into alcohol. Farmers began lighting houses, farms, and businesses and running equipment on the result: free fuel.

> The use of vegetable oils for engine fuels may seem insignificant today. But such oils may become in the course of time as important as petroleum and the coal tar products of the present time.
> —Rudolf Diesel, 1912

Understanding and appreciating the commercial value of our farmers is important for any president, then and now. President Roosevelt felt the American farmer could produce all the food and fuel this country could ever consume, and he was right. They could then, and they can now.

In President Roosevelt's day, petroleum was mostly being used for heating and lighting. Its full potential wouldn't become clear until 1908, when Henry Ford introduced the Model T to the world. America would fall in love with the car and, in so many ways, never be the same again.

The incredible Model T was a flex-fuel automobile, designed to run on either the plant-based fuel called ethanol or a product on the market called petroleum gasoline.

By 1920, millions of automobiles were traveling millions of miles and our nation's farmers were experiencing a huge economic boom in ethanol production and sales. Farmers successfully grew, processed, distributed, and sold the plant-based fuel. Life was looking good for the American family farmer—just before the bottom fell out, anyway. This era would prove to be essentially the last time in history that the American farmer could go to sleep feeling that he could wake up the next morning and still be assured of make a living for his family.

I'm Drowning in a Whiskey River

Eventually, John D. Rockefeller's Standard Oil Company wanted in on this poker game with the farmers and their newfound fortune in fuel. Standard Oil began to sell ethanol at their gas stations across the United States and, practically by sundown, had cornered 25 percent of the farmers' ethanol market. They reduced the price of petroleum gasoline, selling it well below cost. Then, like clockwork, things began to get worse for the American farmer.

In 1920, for whatever reason, Prohibition came along and outlawed all alcohol production in the United States. But this questionable, unpopular law didn't just pertain to whiskey production; congressional rulings also made it illegal for any farmer to brew the new fuel called ethanol, as it required the vegetable or grain to be distilled into alcohol. Every ethanol distillery in the United States was declared illegal and ordered dismantled. When the defiant farmers didn't comply with the national law, they were fined or jailed, or sometimes both. Either way, federal Prohibition agents or their deputies would destroy the ethanol stills on the spot.

One minute the farmers were doing what the president of the United States asked them to do—produce a food-based fuel—and the next minute they were declared outlaws for doing it. Let's ask ourselves what exactly was the result of thirteen years of Prohibition, besides an incredibly dangerous upswing in organized crime? Nearly a quarter million American family farms went under. All we need to do is ask ourselves who could possibly have profited from Prohibition and we'll see the bigger picture of the reasoning behind it.

In 1931, after eleven years of Prohibition and twenty-three years of producing flex-fuel automobiles that could run on either ethanol or gasoline, Henry Ford and the Ford Motor Company stopped building cars that would run on ethanol. Coincidentally, Prohibition ended two years later, in 1933.

So as you can see, today's renewable-fuel movement isn't the first time the American farmer has found himself in direct competition with the big oil companies. But with the seemingly never-ending conflicts in the Middle East and huge oil shortages looming in the near future, this may be the first time in a while that the oil companies have actually needed what the American farmer has to offer: fuel to burn.

To All the Oils I've Loved Before

I thought biodiesel was a well-kept secret when I first began my investigation into alternative fuels, only to find I was light-years behind millions of people who not only had heard of biodiesel—with annual sales of 25 million gallons—but already had a biodiesel infrastructure in place. I did the same thing with Julio Iglesias.

One day I heard Julio singing on the radio, and I was so excited, I wanted to record with him and introduce him to the world. As it turns out, he had already been introduced to the world, and the world had been buying millions of his records for years. Once again, I was the one who needed the introduction.

I also needed to understand a little bit about the business of oil to get an accurate understanding of the business of biodiesel. In 1860, the first year of extensive commercial oil production, 500,000 gallons of rock oil were sold. As a point of reference, in 2005 the world burned 3 billion gallons of oil per day and pumped out 30 billion barrels. With U.S. oil output at the lowest level since the 1950s, we spend more money on oil than any other imported commodity. In this country, we have gone from the first line of Henry Ford's Model Ts to the current number of 130 million cars on the road today.

When it's plentiful, oil can bubble up to the surface of the ground on its own, and you can dig it up with a spoon. They say parts of the Middle East and Africa are like that today. In this country, Native Americans such as the Seneca were smart enough to use it for medicine for centuries. They had a slow, painstaking skimming method of catching the sacred oil. Much later, George Bissell came along and had the unique idea of drilling into the ground to get to the oil, and he hired Edwin L. Drake to do just that. On August 27, 1859, Drake struck oil in Titusville, Pennsylvania, and the United States' first real oil well was born.

When the Seneca Oil Company was formed in 1858 by Bissell and several other investors, oil sold for $40 per barrel. But the inexperienced oil tycoons pumped too much too fast and flooded the market. Oil prices tanked and, after one year, oil dropped to a dime per barrel.

For nearly a decade, the Seneca Oil Company was the only big winner of the high-stakes poker game called the oil business. Then a Mr. Rockefeller wanted to play.

In 1870, John D. Rockefeller began Standard Oil Company with $4,000 of borrowed money. Oil consumption worldwide had grown from 500,000 gallons in 1860 to 20 million barrels per year in 1880. Seneca Oil and other smaller oil companies tried to compete with Standard Oil in this growing market, and Seneca Oil succeeded, but Rockefeller succeeded even more. Then it was the U.S. government's turn to deal.

In 1911, the Supreme Court ruled that Rockefeller had the game locked up and declared Standard Oil Company a monopoly. This forced Rockefeller to divide up Standard Oil and create seven new companies—oil conglomerates that would later become known as the Seven Sisters. Standard Oil of New Jersey eventually changed her name to Exxon; Standard Oil of New York became Mobil; Continental Oil became Conoco; Atlantic Oil would change her name to ARCO; Standard Oil of California became known as Chevron; Standard Oil of Ohio became the U.S. stepsister of British Petroleum; and Standard Oil of Indiana became the U.S. stepsister of Amoco. The Seven Sisters would eventually be called Exxon, Chevron, Texaco, Shell, British Petroleum (BP), Mobil, and Gulf.

Seventy years after Seneca Oil Company overproduced and caused the price of oil to plummet, Texas would discover the largest oil field on record and again flood the market in the process. Outside Beaumont, Texas, on a knoll known as Spindletop, Anthony Lucas and his crew struck oil in a big way. It was the largest gusher to date, and it dramatically changed the landscape of the oil business. Some consider Spindletop the beginning of the modern petroleum industry.

By the 1930s, oil had become more than a personal luxury item; at an annual consumption of 2 billion barrels, it was an immediate necessity. Price stabilization of petroleum was determined to be of national importance, and the U.S. government stepped in and created the Texas Railroad Commission (TRRC). The government authorized the TRRC to shut down production on several Texas oil wells, creating chaos in the fields. Martial law was declared, and troops were brought in to keep order. Sometimes order just doesn't want to be kept, and many of the oil companies smuggled out the oil anyway.

Today's oil business has changed considerably since the Texas wildcatting days, when you operated on a hunch and a hope—the hope of striking it rich merely by drilling a hole in the ground. Now, equipment can tell exactly where a well should and should not be drilled; but I don't hear bells ringing and whistles blowing signaling too many new gushers. Researchers say 65 to 70 percent of oil today comes from fields discovered before 1970 and 80 to 90 percent of the planet's remaining oil has already been discovered.

Turn Out the Lights, the Party's Over

According to the Energy Information Administration, the United States consumes 125 billion gallons of gasoline per year and 60 billion gallons of diesel and ethanol per year. Three billion gallons of petroleum are burned daily in one form or another. At our peak, we produced 11 million gallons per day. It's hardly debated that the Earth's supply of petroleum-based oil will be exhausted within the next fifty years. In 1956, geologist M. King Hubbert accurately predicted for his bosses at Shell Oil Company that the Texas-U.S. oil supply would peak in 1970–71, and it did. This led to the prolific scientific prediction "Where goes Texas, so goes the planet."

Some say, Drill in Alaska, we've still got oil! But who actually profits from that besides the oil companies? Not America, not in the long run. Not at a one cent per gallon savings at the pump; according to experts, that's all drilling in Alaska will bring us, besides environmental devastation and pollution. We can't trade in the pristine beauty of our last expanse of wilderness for the possibility of a fantasy decade or two of cheaper oil. The price of oil goes up at the drop of a hat, no matter where you're pulling it out of the ground or how much we really have under there. Just look at today's newspapers.

Right now, half of the existing pipeline in Alaska is shut off or broken-down completely, causing oil prices to soar. Then there's the huge new offshore oil field recently discovered in the Gulf of Mexico. That discovery would have sounded more promising had we not just gone through a Category 5 hurricane (Katrina) in that same gulf.

In the 1950s, the Seven Sisters set the price of oil. At the present time, only four sisters are remaining: BP, Shell,

Exxon/Mobil, and Chevron/Texaco. I've also heard them referred to in the business as Kathy, Janet, Dianne, and Peggy. No, I take that back, that's the Lennon Sisters ... my mistake.

These days, one rash decision from the Organization of the Petroleum Exporting Countries (OPEC) and we're paying double at the pumps. Drilling for Alaskan oil is no permanent solution. Why ruin the last real frontier in America by drilling in Alaska? That oil will certainly run out eventually. Then what? Are we like desperate teenagers thoughtlessly selling Grandpa's treasured gold watch the second we're broke? Are immature minds considering only our immediate needs with no thought of the long-term consequences?

Middle Eastern oil is no permanent solution. Gulf oil is not the solution. Fossil fuels are not the solution, no matter what country they come from. Not when wars have to be fought to secure the rights. Not when the emissions are killing people. Not when wildlife and ecosystems are disturbed or destroyed forever. Not when all we have to do is grow our own fuel crops instead of burning fossil fuels. We need to conserve our natural resources, not continue to search for new ways to waste them.

I Get My Energy from the Sun

Mother Earth has remarkably produced enough oil to amply serve the hungry planet, but no feast lasts forever. Folks disagree on how much oil we still have, what's the best way to go get it, where not to get it, or how using it is affecting the planet. No one can argue this fact of life: when it's gone, it's gone.

If you think about it, all energy on Earth comes from the Sun in one way or another. Oil is basically hydrogen and carbon, or hydrocarbons. Hydrocarbons are stored energy from the Sun, so oil is just another form of solar energy. When you burn oil, hydrocarbons give off light and heat—light and heat that was stored from the Sun.

Because the laws of nature still prevail, by all estimates we'll eventually come to the end of Mother Earth's generous portions of fossil fuels. This will create a catastrophic energy crisis if we're not prepared, and the laws of physics dictate that energy cannot be created or destroyed, only changed. It's time to concentrate on the only thing we can do: change.

Part II: The Future

Yesterday's Wine

I sensibly waited to be born until Prohibition was lifted in 1933. My parents lived with my grandparents in the tiny cotton-farming community of Abbott, Texas. I come from an extensive family background in transportation. My father was a Ford mechanic and my grandfather was the town blacksmith. Our family relied heavily on good horsepower.

I guess Daddy Nelson knew that his profession of blacksmithing probably wouldn't carry me very far. Before my grandfather died when I was six years old, he bought me a guitar, taught me a few chords, and sent me out into the world with a profession that would last me a lifetime. I can never thank him enough.

Growing up, my sister, Bobbie, and I sure picked our share of cotton. We had a cotton gin in Abbott, so our loads didn't have far to travel. Abbott cotton was planted, picked, and processed right there in town. The cotton was then taken a few miles down the road to the Corsicana Cotton Mill, where it was spun into thread, placed on spools, and taken to the textile mills in Fort Worth. All this was accomplished within a fifty-mile radius. From seed to store within fifty miles—that's the efficient way. Today, we might grow the cotton in one state, truck it to another for ginning, another for the mills, and yet another for distribution. That cotton has traveled 1,000 road miles before it makes it to the consumer. Think how far the imported goods have to travel, shipped thousands of miles, consuming hundreds of gallons of fuel, when all we had to do was produce it locally like we used to do in Abbott.

I'd like to see biodiesel and ethanol processed within a few feet of the fields where the crops were grown. The key to efficiency is going to have to be localized production. Why use up 50 gallons of biodiesel to transport 1,000 gallons of biodiesel to the consumer?

Like Daddy Nelson, I believe in everyone doing what they're good at. Why can't Texas grow what it's already producing (cotton and corn, among others) and Idaho grow what it grows (potatoes and wheat) and process the alternative fuels right on the spot? I can see a future where biodiesel plants and ethanol plants work side by side, producing both forms of renewable fuels simultaneously. Farmers can deliver their loads of vegetables, plants, or tallow to the fuel-processing plants each day, and for fueling the trip back home, all they have to do is fill up their tanks with biodiesel or ethanol made from yesterday's crops. How simple can it be?

> The diesel engine can be fed with vegetable oils and would help considerably in the development of agriculture of the countries which use it.
> —Rudolf Diesel, 1911

Not only farming communities have crops to burn; even urban areas produce a biodiesel fuel crop: yellow grease. Think of the millions of gallons of yellow grease that restaurants throw away in large cities such as Dallas, Houston, Los Angeles, and New York. But the yellow grease program doesn't just have to be for restaurants. I read an article this year that explained how Thailand is successfully experimenting with a new yellow grease program in which customers can sell their used cooking oil from home at their local service stations. The money is dispensed within minutes or traded for biodiesel. Again, how simple can it be?

Petroleum versus Biodiesel

Mother Earth's Recipe for Petroleum

Ingredients:

170 quadrillion tons algae

252 billion tons (approximately) dinosaurs

1 dash or sprinkling of various other prehistoric animals
and vegetation (chef's choice)

Instructions:

In a very large cooking pan, also known as an ocean, cover
ingredients generously with warm salty water. All algae,
dinosaurs, and vegetation will eventually settle to the
bottom, creating a roux.

Cover completely with heavy layers of silt, shale, and muck.

Cook at 400 degrees for 100 million years.

The mixture will eventually turn into a hard rock, and,
when stirred, an oily substance will bubble out. Cover
the oil with a piece of sandstone (if sandstone isn't
available, any porous rock will do). Next, cover the oily
sandstone with a clean nonpermeable rock and simmer
continuously for another 200 million years, stirring
occasionally.

Yield: At least 2 trillion barrels oil*

*Note: May be difficult and costly to remove from pan

Petroleum-based oil takes millions of years to create and millions of dollars to get out of the ground. Biodiesel can be made at home in a blender in less than thirty minutes. This is especially nice if you drive a diesel skateboard to work. Otherwise, you'll probably need a bigger batch. Plus, a person could blow up their kitchen and ruin the engine in their car if he's not careful. It's definitely best to leave biodiesel production to the professionals. But if you're brave and have good insurance, here's how it's done:

Willie's Blender Biodiesel

Prep time: 20 minutes

Clean up: Varies considerably

Ingredients:

200 milliliters methanol (Caution: can make you go blind)

3.5 grams lye

1 liter vegetable oil

Instructions:

Place methanol and lye in blender. Blend. Stop. Blend some more. You have now created sodium methoxide. The sides of the blender should be getting hot. At this point, the mixture can eat through your skin and the fumes are explosive and dangerous to inhale. Have the fire extinguisher and a telephone handy.

Pour vegetable oil in with the sodium methoxide. Blend for 15 minutes. Cheaper blenders can and will fall apart during this process of continuous blending. I like to sing to the mixture right about now. Any good country song will do—something with a good beat. Stop blending and singing after 15 minutes. If done correctly, two layers will form. The bottom layer is glycerin, a by-product of the procedure, and the other layer is biodiesel. The glycerin can be safely composted or made into soap to clean up the mess in the kitchen.

Yield: I liter biodiesel

Enjoy!

The process of making biodiesel is called transesterification. There was a time when I couldn't even spell transesterification, much less know what it meant. Actually, I still can't spell it, but at least I do know what it means: brewing bio.

Inside the vegetable oil, molecules called triglycerides are made up of several groups of long-chain trans-fatty acids. Under the microscope, you can see that the chains are grouped in threes, like a musical trio. A single glycerin molecule anchors each group of three chains, much like a lead singer would anchor the trio. When methanol is added to the vegetable oil, it causes the glycerin to separate and release from the long-chain fatty acids. This forms two distinct layers: one layer of glycerin and one layer of loose, long-chain fatty acids, called biodiesel. You might say that Glycerin, the lead singer for the Triglycerides, has a reaction to the methanol music and breaks away from the trio to go out on his own. The remaining chains form a new group, name themselves Biodiesel, and are immediately destined for stardom. That's transesterification.

> Hey good lookin', whatcha got cookin? How's about cookin' somethin' up with me?
> —Hank Williams

So now that I've told you how to make biodiesel, I suppose I should explain a little bit more about exactly what it is. If you really want to get technical …

bio•die•sel (bī´ō dē´z&l, s&l), *n.* a fuel composed of mono-alkyl esters of long-chain fatty acids derived from vegetable oils or animal fats, and in accordance with standards specified by the designated B100 fuel and meeting the requirements of the American Society for Testing and Materials D6751 specification.

If you ask the National Biodiesel Board, they'll describe biodiesel as "a clean-burning alternative fuel produced from domestic, renewable resources. Biodiesel contains no petroleum but can be blended at any level with petroleum diesel to create a biodiesel blend. It can be used in compression ignition (diesel) engines with no major modifications. Biodiesel is simple to use, biodegradable, nontoxic, and essentially free of sulfur and aromatics."

Any way you slice it, biodiesel is a feasible alternative energy source.

Here's a sampling of the advantages of using biodiesel:

- Biodiesel reduces carbon dioxide exhaust emissions by over 78 percent.
- Biodiesel produces no sulfur dioxide (the major cause of acid rain). Petroleum does.
- Biodiesel reduces exhaust smoke emissions by up to 55 percent. The black cloud associated with a diesel engine can be eliminated by using biodiesel.
- Biodiesel smells good!
- Biodiesel is less dangerous. with a lower flash point than diesel. In addition, because of its low flash point, it is classified in the fire code as the same as vegetable oil or milk (Class III-B liquid).
- Biodiesel degrades four times faster than petroleum diesel.
- Biodiesel provides significant lubricity improvement over petroleum-based diesel fuel, thus extending the life of the engine.
- Biodiesel reduces the classic diesel engine "knocking" noise.
- Biodiesel can be used in any tank or storage facility right away.
- Biodiesel can be mixed with existing diesel to create any level of blend. A diesel engine needs little or no modification to use biodiesel. Some older vehicles may require rubber hoses and gaskets to be replaced with synthetic ones.

Sometimes It's Heaven, Sometimes It's Hell

With every positive comes a little negative, and biodiesel is no exception. While the positive attributes greatly outweigh the negative, I feel the negative require at least an honorable mention.

Insufficient availability. Biodiesel can be expensive to produce, with processing plants costing millions of dollars. This limits the number of refineries, which in turn limits the availability of biodiesel. More and more biodiesel tanks are popping up all over the country, making biodiesel easier and easier to purchase, but we've got a long way to go before we can drive from Maine to California on biodiesel that we leisurely bought at the pump.

Climate sensitivity. One-hundred-percent biodiesel can gel up in the winter months, clogging the vehicle's fuel system. The cold-flow troubles are avoided by using a blend of at least 80 percent diesel and 20 percent biodiesel (B20), the official suggested blend recommended for colder climates.

Contamination. The fuel quality isn't always uniform from city to city. Fuel can leave the plant in perfect condition and, because of the number of people handling it, become contaminated on the way to the pump. Although the National Biodiesel Accreditation Commission sets the strict standards known as BQ-9000 (a series of procedures that are followed to avoid contamination), not all biodiesel producers are accredited. For quality assurance, always look for the BQ-9000 stamp of approval and buy only from accredited dealers.

Rubber breakdown. Biodiesel cleans the engine, acting as a solvent. This unique solvent ability can also ruin the rubber hoses and other rubber parts in older fuel systems.

Rubber must be replaced with synthetic hoses, gaskets, and seals. Newer vehicles are already equipped with synthetic materials at the factory and require no adaptation at all.

Warranties. There's a difference between straight vegetable oil (SVO) and biodiesel. SVO has not been through the transesterification process, so the glycerin is still attached to the three long chains of fatty acids. When heated at high temperatures, the glycerin polymerizes like plastic. Using SVO as diesel engine fuel will void some vehicle warranties, so check before you install any of the SVO adjustment kits available on the market. Just because you *can* run your diesel engine on SVO doesn't necessarily mean you *should*. For better results, use biodiesel instead.

There's a Home Place Under Fire Tonight in the Heartland

During the Live Aid concert in 1985, Bob Dylan said we needed to also help this country's dwindling number of family farmers. I took what he said seriously, and that following year we had our first Farm Aid benefit concert in Champaign, Illinois. I had hoped that we'd have one large concert, draw attention to the problems the family farmers were facing, and the matter would eventually be settled with money and public support and awareness. That was more than twenty years ago, and we still have to have Farm Aid concerts every year. Although the United States continues to lose more than 500 family farms a week, Neil Young, John Mellencamp, Dave Matthews, and I have not given up hope, and we are constantly trying to raise public awareness and needed money for the backbone of our country: the American family farmer.

Family farmers are small farmers who love the land. They're still not getting enough money for their product and are rapidly losing their battle to stay in business. By helping the American family farmer, we will in turn help ourselves out of the economic hole that we find ourselves in today. It doesn't really matter how we got here; the point is, we have to dig our way out.

Biodiesel seems to be the answer to a lot of our prayers. Not only can it help the U.S. economy, our unwanted dependence on foreign oil, and the gasping environment, it could also help the family farmers out of this tragic dilemma they have found themselves in through no fault of their own.

I've Been Everywhere, Man

There are 28 million heavy-duty diesel vehicles in the United States today. I'll bet you that I have probably passed every one of them at one time or another during my sixty years on the road. I don't know how many miles my band and I have traveled; no one really adds it up. I do know I've gone through several airplanes, buses, trucks, vans, and cars throughout my career as an entertainer. Between my regular touring schedule, benefits, movies, television, and recording projects,

> Of travel, I've had my share, man, I've been everywhere.
> —Hank Snow

I usually work 300 days per year. We're never in the same place more than one or two days. America's roads are my driveway, and my house is my bus. And I wouldn't have it any other way.

Because of the many miles we put on our vehicles out here on the road, I felt it was the perfect testing and research opportunity for biodiesel. I could see firsthand how the product worked for the consumer. I told Gates, Tony, Johnny, and Neal, our bus drivers, that I wanted them to start filling up with 100 percent biodiesel wherever and whenever possible, no matter what it cost. In the beginning it was very hard to find biodiesel. We'd look on the National Biodiesel Board's Web site regularly to find new places to purchase it.

Many times we'd call a licensed distributor and they'd bring it out to the buses wherever we were, either at the hotels or the gig. Sometimes they'd be there with the usual large silver oil tank pulled by a semi. But a lot of times they'd show up with big barrels of biodiesel in the back of a pickup or van. Once, several young people showed up in an old school bus. They just pulled out a hose and started pumping. By the time we'd all had our pictures taken together, the bus was filled up with what turned out to be the best fuel on the road yet, and we were on our way to the next town. How simple could it be?

In the beginning, biodiesel was more expensive than diesel, especially if you're like me and have the distributor deliver it to your tank. Congress recently passed a dollar-per-gallon incentive tax reduction, or credit, for producers, making biodiesel and diesel just about equal in price. We were in Michigan the other day, and biodiesel was much cheaper than diesel fuel. Hopefully for us, the consumer, this represents a trend. I know my truck-driving buddies feel the same.

The School of Hard NO$_x$

Whenever you burn anything, nitrogen is emitted. Some biofuels emit more nitrogen oxides (NO$_x$) than others because they burn hotter, depending on the feedstock. Some cars emit more NO$_x$ than others because they're older. The individual results of NO$_x$ tests can differ considerably. Testing NO$_x$ results on several feedstocks for 100 percent biodiesel has also varied; some NO$_x$ levels were higher than petroleum, some lower than petroleum.

NO_x emissions in biodiesel can be greatly reduced to levels well below those of regular diesel by using additives. The amount of reduction depends on the additive and the original feedstock used to produce the biodiesel. Nationwide, automatically blending biodiesel with our existing diesel fuel supply could bring dramatic reductions in NO_x emissions, without the need to retrofit any vehicles or fueling infrastructures.

As far as smog is concerned, it's the levels of volatile organic compounds (VOCs) that must be addressed, not the NO_x emissions. Biodiesel has very low levels of VOCs; therefore, it doesn't contribute to smog levels like petroleum-based fuels do.

Without proper lubrication, today's diesel engine will not operate efficiently. Regular diesel fuel has a very low lubricity level, and, until recently, sulfur was generously added to help increase lubrication. We eventually realized that sulfur is the number-one cause of acid rain and that it contributes to the destruction of the ozone. This is not to be confused with the destruction of the end zone, which I'll cover in my next manuscript, *The Glory Days of a Rabid Abbott Panther.*

> The use of B20 biodiesel could remove 24,000 tons of NO_x from the air in Texas every year.
> —National Biodiesel Board

After decades of environmental destruction, thankfully, all U.S. diesel fuel is finally being switched to ultra-low-sulfur diesel (ULSD). The Environmental Protection Agency (EPA) ruled that all sulfur levels in diesel gasoline must be reduced from the original accepted 500 ppm to 15 ppm, therefore reducing sulfur levels by more than 95 percent by the end of 2007. Because sulfur was mainly added to petroleum diesel fuel for its lubrication capabilities, ULSD will need a replacement for the sulfur. This is another possible venue for biodiesel.

Vegetable oil's lubricity levels are extremely high, making biodiesel a much better choice for a clean, nontoxic diesel fuel additive. Biodiesel makes an excellent additive for petroleum diesel, and a blend of only 2 percent biodiesel can significantly increase the life expectancy of America's 28 million heavy-duty diesel vehicles merely by increasing the lubricity of the fuel burned while also complying with the newest EPA regulations.

Through the years, biodiesel test results have surely varied, but most tests concluded the following: in the long run, in every way, biodiesel is better for the environment than petroleum diesel. In 1996, the U.S. Department of Energy and the Department of Transportation recognized these test results and designated 100 percent biodiesel (B100) as an alternative fuel. Now it's just a matter of it catching on with consumers, suppliers, and industries.

On May 16, 2005, President George W. Bush spoke in West Point, Virginia, at the Virginia BioDiesel Refinery and said, "Biodiesel is one of our nation's most promising alternative fuel sources, and by developing biodiesel, you're making this country less dependent on foreign sources of oil. Biodiesel burns more completely and produces less air pollution than gasoline or regular diesel. Biodiesel can also reduce engine wear, and produces almost no sulfur emissions, which makes it a good choice for cities and states working to meet strict air quality standards."

I'm glad to see that President Bush agrees with me on this one; this country has become too reliant on foreign oil, and biodiesel is a good, safe, reliable alternative choice for an independent, better America.

As evidenced by Prohibition, the government hasn't always considered the better choice. Under protest, in 1994 the government signed on to the North American Free Trade Agreement (NAFTA) and drove yet another nail in the awaiting coffin of the American family farmer. Under NAFTA, world imports of fruits, vegetables, grains, and beef increased tremendously, not only leading to a widening trade deficit but also diminishing the value of U.S. goods. Within two years of NAFTA, the price of U.S. wheat fell 56 percent and the price of U.S. corn fell 46 percent. The value of every U.S. bulk commodity export plummeted. Sure, the quantity of some of our exports went up for a while (exports to Canada and Mexico went up 150 percent), but our imports from Canada and Mexico also went up. For example, Mexican beef imports increased by 1,000 percent. Whatever trade balance we ever had was toppled.

> If you've got the money, honey, I've got the time.
> —Lefty Frizzell

Somebody might want to rethink the idea that we're saving money by outsourcing our jobs to other countries and importing goods that appear to be cheaper but really cost us more in the long run. Besides the loss of millions of valuable jobs, the U.S. national trade deficit for 2005 was officially listed as $805 billion. Two billion dollars of that deficit can be attributed to oil imports, but the majority represents imports of goods from China. At this rate, we will soon reach a trillion-dollar trade deficit. This enormous negative dollar figure eventually weakens the strength of U.S. currency, in turn weakening the U.S. economy. A weak economy can be devastating not only for the family farmer, but every other hard-working American as well. The working class is the foundation of this country. The more the U.S. dollar and the U.S. economy suffer, the more the people who hold up the framework of this nation will suffer. Something needs to be done to pull us out of this downward spiral.

The three major crops in the United States, our bulk commodities, currently are soybeans, corn, and wheat, with beef coming up quickly at a close fourth place. All of these crops are excellent candidates for either bio-diesel or ethanol production, or sometimes both. Corn, for instance, can produce ethanol or biodiesel. As I research and dig a little deeper into the wonders of renewable fuels, I'm amazed at the amount of natural sources for biodiesel. Not only does almost any vegetable or plant (over 350 species) make an excellent potential source for biodiesel, but the stems and stalks can also be baled and processed into fuel. Yes, grasses can become gasses. Even algae can be processed and used for biodiesel.

As far as other crops are concerned, palm oil yields 635 gallons of biodiesel per acre per year; coconut oil yields 290 gallons; rapeseed yields 125 gallons; mustard yields 65 gallons; sunflowers yield 100 gallons; peanuts yield 115 gallons; soybeans yield 50 gallons; canola (rapeseed's niece) yields 50 gallons; cotton yields 35 gallons; oats yield 25 gallons; and corn yields 20 gallons per acre per year. Yields may vary depending on weather, climate, and region.

Another natural hydrocarbon source is animal fat, or tallow. The meat industry's slaughterhouses reportedly generate over a billion gallons of grease and tallow per year. Tallow can also be easily converted into energy-efficient, clean-burning biodiesel. Currently, we use three-quarters of the grease and tallow, which is inedible for humans, for animal feed. This practice is illegal in Europe, and soon those laws will transfer to the United States. The United States Department of Agriculture has offered $50 million in loan guarantees for new livestock-waste biofuel projects.

You've also got yellow grease from used cooking oils,

brown grease from grease traps, and even black grease (sludge) from sewage plants; all are excellent bases for biodiesel.

The next steps are to sort out the cost-prohibitive sources from the cost-effective sources of biofuels. Some sources of biodiesel have higher oil content than others, and some feedstocks are more expensive to bring to the tank than they're worth. Algae has the highest oil content of all potential sources and requires the least amount of land to deliver, but it costs the most to produce, not only in dollars but in energy spent to retrieve the oil. Algae yields 9,000 gallons of oil per year per acre but requires a billion-dollar processing plant. Nine million acres of algae could fuel the nation, but the fuel would require trillions of dollars to produce. Practicality must come into play.

Pick Up the Tempo

Production of biofuels in 2005 equaled nearly 2 percent of world fuel use. From 2000 to 2005, ethanol production worldwide nearly tripled, growing from 4.6 billion to 12.2 billion gallons. Biodiesel climbed to an estimated 790 million gallons in 2005 from 251 million gallons in 2000. Thankfully, the use of biodiesel is growing rapidly in the United States, partly due to increased legislation requiring reductions in ozone-depleting particulates released into the air by burning fossil fuels such as petroleum, natural gas, or coal. Many government fleets already operate on 100 percent biodiesel or ethanol or a blend of petroleum and renewable fuels.

Environmentally pleasing government actions have left the doors wide open for a fuel-hungry nation to hop aboard the renewable-fuels train. The United States' great minds have gone to work, and within a very short time, millions of consumers will begin—if they haven't already—quitting their oil addictions, asking intelligent renewable-fuel questions, purchasing flex-fuel vehicles, switching from diesel to biodiesel or from gas to ethanol, becoming proactive in their community, and coming up with brilliant solutions to our existing fuel crisis.

Tremendous strides have been made in terms of understanding biodiesel and broadening its consumer acceptance in this country. I would have to say the turning point had to be the passing of the Energy Policy Act (EPAct) in 1992, after years of resistance. The goal of the EPAct is a 10 percent reduction of U.S. petroleum consumption by the year 2000 (didn't happen) and a 30 percent reduction by 2010 (still could happen).

Federal and state agencies will attempt to reduce their petroleum consumption by 35 percent by 2010. Existing government gasoline- and diesel-burning fleets will eventually be replaced by newer flex-fuel vehicles. In 1998, the EPAct was amended and new rulings were handed down allowing government agencies to use renewable fuels such as ethanol and biodiesel in their existing vehicles instead of being required to purchase new vehicles in order to remain in compliance.

Thanks to the biodiesel rule of 1998, agencies can meet up to 50 percent of their fleet requirements by burning a blend of B20 or higher. Agencies can trade out credits for burning 2,220 gallons of B20 in their existing diesel vehicles in lieu of having to purchase one new flex-fuel vehicle.

The American Jobs Creation Act of 2004 (JOBS Bill) brought a tax incentive for biodiesel producers and blenders, allowing them to compete with the price of petroleum diesel. The excise-tax credit gives the biodiesel blenders a one cent per percentage point tax credit for agriculture-

There are many government agencies and other organized efforts that are making use of biodiesel and other alternative fuels. Here are a few examples:

- The Clean Cities Program offers incentives and grant money for the purchase of alternative-fuel vehicles.
- The Clean School Bus USA program reduces children's exposure to harmful petroleum diesel fumes. More than 100 school districts nationwide have voluntarily made the switch to biodiesel. Las Vegas school districts have used biodiesel in their school buses for more than ten years.
- The U.S. Navy uses 1 million gallons of B20 per year, more biodiesel than any other group in the United States.
- The U.S. Post Office uses over 250,000 gallons of B100 yearly.
- NASA uses biofuels in all available vehicles.
- A quarter of all states have implemented tax incentives to lower the price of biodiesel and increase biodiesel production.
- Minnesota's legislature voted in mandatory biodiesel use statewide. All diesel sold must be at least a 2 percent biodiesel blend, and all gasoline must contain at least 10 percent ethanol. Michigan has similar legislation.
- Hawaii cut state taxes in half for all biofuels.
- Shell Oil Company has pledged billions of dollars for biofuel research and development.
- There are over 5 million flex-fuel vehicles on the road in the United States.
- Chrysler fills its new diesel vehicles with a biodiesel blend at the factory.
- All new John Deere tractors come from the factory with a B2 blend of biodiesel in the tank.
- My alma mater, Baylor University, has a program to study the use of sludge (black grease) as a biodiesel feedstock for a possible aviation fuel.
- In the spirit of Rudolf Diesel, the University of Georgia has a biodiesel program in operation using a feedstock of peanuts.

- In Montana, camelina (a member of the mustard family) is being studied as a possible biodiesel feedstock.
- Michigan introduced legislation requiring a mandatory minimum 2 percent blend in all diesel sold.
- Biofuels workshops are available in nearly every state.

based biodiesel (canola, soy, cotton, and so forth).

Whenever we're on the road across the United States, we always try to get 100 percent biodiesel for our cars, trucks, and buses. When we are able to find it, we're confident that the fuel we're buying is top quality, because government regulations are very strict. When we are able to find fuel that comes from a BQ-9000 certified marketer, we're confident that it's top-shelf. The government and industry are very supportive of the BQ-9000 quality-control system. You must be accredited if you intend to sell the biodiesel you have produced. This protects the consumer. In other words, it's legal to grow it, you just can't sell it. Not without a permit, anyway.

There are many new commercial biodiesel producers in this country, and most are very professional and dedicated to the cause. People like my friends Bob and Kelly King are building and operating some of the United States' finest biodiesel refineries and are respected experts when it comes to the complex biorefineries necessary for extensive commercial biodiesel production. A biodiesel refinery can cost as much as $1 per every gallon of biodiesel produced in one year. A 100-million-gallon-per-year plant can cost $100 million to build. The Kings' award-winning company, Pacific Biodiesel, has built biodiesel plants in Japan, Hawaii, Virginia, Oregon, Nevada, Pennsylvania, Maryland, and, more recently, the new biodiesel plant in Carl's Corner, Texas, near my hometown of Abbott.

There are also many people devoted to the research and development of biodiesel. By the time I first heard the word *biodiesel*, Charles Peterson, a professor emeritus of biological and agricultural engineering at the University of Idaho, had already started a biodiesel research program and had been at it for more than twenty years. Since 1979, Professor Peterson and the university have supported the idea of alternative energy and America's farmers growing fuel. In terms of research, testing, and development, the University of Idaho has rightfully earned the reputation as a respected leader in the unplowed field of biodiesel research and education. Peterson writes:

> Vegetable oil has potential as an alternative energy source. However, vegetable oil alone will not solve our dependence on foreign oil. Use of this and other alternative energy sources could contribute to a more stable supply of energy. Major production centers have not been developed; however, the number of plants is expanding and many additional ones are under study.
>
> The magnitude of our energy needs provides an inexhaustible market for our total agricultural production capacity at the highest possible level. We could put the farm back to work providing for our food needs and also growing crops and livestock for energy. Energy is the only crop that could never grow in surplus.

BioWillie

My friends Dennis Weaver and Darryl Hannah were the first entertainers I knew about who were actively using and promoting biodiesel. They ran their personal vehicles and ranch equipment on it and spoke about biodiesel throughout the

United States. They believed in protecting the environment while supporting the American farmer. I quickly realized they were on to something wonderful for our future, and I shared their concern about our country's complete reliance on petroleum for fuel and their passion about the need to support the farmers. I knew I needed to help them get the word out. So I bought a biodiesel company.

I have always believed in putting your money where your mouth is, and in this case, my money's on biodiesel. I wanted to let folks know that I wouldn't ask them to believe in something that I wouldn't invest in myself. Near my hometown of Abbott, my partners and I at Texas Biodiesel are building a biodiesel processing plant. I also teamed up with Earth Biofuels, and, at the same location, we've built a new truck stop. Morgan Freeman and I broke ground on April 1, 2006. The truck stop, known as Willie's Place at Carl's Corner, Texas, is now open, and once completed, the biodiesel facility will process 2 million gallons of biodiesel per year and serve much of central Texas.

Every Wednesday afternoon at 1:00 P.M. CST, I appear on a live call-in radio show on channel 171 on XM Satellite Radio. I call in to my friend disc jockey Bill Mack's *Open Road* radio show, and they hook me up so the public can hear me. Truckers from all over the United States call in on Willie Wednesdays, and we talk about the road, talk that lately includes the subject of biodiesel.

When we first started the program a couple of years ago, the truckers' questions regarding biodiesel were much different. Those truckers were more inquisitive than the ones who call these days. By now, they are becoming more educated on the subject, having tested the product themselves. At first, they were like me; they'd never even heard of biodiesel. Now, not only have they tried out biodiesel, they seem to have more information than I do sometimes, especially when it comes to biodiesel's availability throughout the country.

I love my hour each week with the truck drivers and look forward to Wednesdays. Here are some transcripts of a few of my favorite Willie Wednesdays when the topic turned to biodiesel.

Date: January 25, 2005

Bill Mack: Ladies and gentleman, here's Willie Nelson … in wonderful Luck, Texas.

I was talking about a new product that is coming out that has really caught my attention, Willie Nelson's Biodiesel. We talked about this yesterday. Somebody called and wanted to know if that was the smoke coming out of your bus. Is it because you use this Willie Nelson Biodiesel? Yeah, somebody sent a note about that yesterday.

Willie Nelson: That's pretty funny. Tell them not to be so funny. I accepted an environmental award a few days ago out in California, and Woody Harrelson introduced me and everything. I was telling them that my wife and I both drive biodiesel automobiles and that it was very safe fuel. I said, "The other night, I pulled my car in the garage, closed the door, went to sleep, and left the motor running. I woke up the next morning and I'd gained five pounds."

Bill: Let's get serious here. We'll open up the telephone lines and let some of you people talk to this man here. Tell me about it. I knew this was coming because you discussed it on one of my shows here. Willie Nelson Biodiesel. It's a fuel that will be at truck stops, and it's made from vegetable oils, mainly soybeans, that can be burned without modification to diesel engines. That sounds great, Will.

Willie: Yeah, it is a great idea. There's a lot more than soybeans. In fact, the original diesel engine was designed to run on peanut oil, so there's a whole range of products a farmer can grow that we can really use. First of all, we'll save the agricultural business, save the small family farmer, and keep us from being so dependent on foreign energy.

Bill: I had a lad call in saying thank you for all you do for farmers. Just a few minutes ago. This is something. We have plenty of oil if you use a product like this. Then there's no shortage of finding the fuel for the diesels.

Willie: Well, yeah. If our school buses were to start burning biodiesel, it would be so much healthier for the kids and the drivers because of the air. Biodiesel is environmentally friendly to the air, as opposed to gasoline and regular diesel.

Bill: Alright now. Of course, this is a question I don't think you can answer yet. I know that Love's truck stops and you are talking to some of the truck stops, and now [biodiesel] will be available. How long do you think it will be before drivers can get this product anywhere? I'm talking about geographically, anywhere they are traveling.

Willie: Well, fortunately, it's getting easier. In fact, our drivers have places where they can stop between here and L.A. We fill up here at the ranch, first of all. We have a 600-gallon tank back here where I can fill up my buses before I leave. Then, by the time we get to Carl's Corner, I can fill up again or top it off. We stop at other places heading west. I think Tucson we can stop and we get 100 percent, or 80/20, or whatever we need, depending on the weather. The real cold weather a lot of truckers like the B20, but either way, it's a great improvement over 100 percent regular diesel, which is not environmental friendly, and it's, first of all, getting higher. We're running out of it.

Bill: Good answer there. Let's talk to somebody. We'll talk to some people then take a break and get back to one-on-one with Will.

[**Commercial break**]

Bill: Temptation ... are you there? You want to meet Willie? This is Temptation.

Temptation: Hi, Willie.

Willie: Hello. How ya doin'?

Tempt: Great. I have to tell you something. I have been in love with you for, oh, probably twenty-five years now.

[...]

Willie: Well, that's great. I feel like we are bonded in some way.

Tempt: I have a question about your biodiesel. Now, does that mix with the diesel?

Willie: Well, you can mix it in. We're running 100 percent biodiesel in my buses, and some truckers like to run B20, especially up in the northern country, where the weather is colder. They say it burns better and doesn't get so thick. They are working on ways in that part of the country to get it so you can run 100 percent biodiesel up there.

Tempt: Okay. 'Cause I run out of Spokane, Washington, up in the Northwest. It does get a little chilly.

Willie: B20, I hear from the drivers, is really good, and they love it.

Tempt: Okay, great. Keep up the good work.

Willie: Thanks.

Bill: Thank you, Temptation. Link, where you calling from? Link?

Link: Will, how are ya?

Willie: I'm fine. How are you? Who's this?

Link: This is Link.

Willie: Hey, Link.

Link: Bill, you ask me where I am. I'm sitting in a TA [TravelCenters of America] in Sydney. No, not Sydney, I'm in Ohio somewhere.

Willie: That's good. I'm in Texas somewhere.

Link: You live in Austin. I know where you're at.

Willie: Yeah, I'm in Luck, Texas, which is a little bit west of Austin and slightly higher.

Link: I won't go there, Willie.

Bill: What's your question, pal?

Link: I heard a rumor, Willie, that you're buying Carl's Corner [Truck Stop].

Willie: Well, I won it in a poker game. So now I don't know whether to keep it going or try to lose it back, but it seems like a good opportunity to promote biodiesel [and] good organic food. I don't think there's ever been a 100 percent organic restaurant for truckers. Also, it's got a great place in the back for some entertainment. I'm going to have maybe some live concerts and maybe we can broadcast them on XM.

Link: That would be great.

[…]

Thank you very much, Willie.

Bill: Thank you, Link. … We got a guy named Ken. Ken, where you calling from, pal?

Ken: I'm in about ten miles from the Colorado border. I'm in Utah on I-70.

Bill: Talk to Willie.

Willie: Hey, Ken. How ya doin'?

Ken: Good. I'm proud to hear that you're working with biodiesel. I've been a farmer most all my life. I drive a truck in the wintertime. Your work with the concerts for the farmers, that's real good. Glad to hear about that.

Willie: Well, thank you. We got into it several years ago, thinking that once the people in power realized that the family farmer was in trouble they would do something about it, but unfortunately, they haven't. We've had to do Farm Aid nineteen years now, or twenty years, so we're still doing them. The problem is still there. I think biodiesel could be the answer. I think we need to get our government to back our farmers to grow fuel and feed our country so we don't have to go around fighting wars over oil.

Ken: Yes. I agree 100 percent, and I'm going to try to use it on my farm as well.

Willie: Great. It runs in all diesel engines. You really don't have to do anything to it, and you can run a tank of regular diesel and a tank of biodiesel if you can't find it, so that's a handy thing. […]

Bill: I tell ya what. Willie has helped the farmers so much. The new biodiesel coming out, Willie Nelson Biodiesel … I have a feeling it's going to be the answer to so many problems, not only with the engines of the vehicles but overall, it's going to benefit so many. We'll talk more about that later. Willie Nelson is on the show. Could not ask for a nicer guest. … We're going to catch up on phone calls here. You brought up a subject a while ago about Carl's Corner, Texas, which is not too far from us. I call it Hillsboro, but it's down the road from Hillsboro.

Willie: Eight miles north of Hillsboro, I think, or something in that neighborhood. Exit 374 at I-35.

Bill: You'll have the product there that we've been talking about. I can't stress enough how this has caught the attention of people. Willie Nelson's Biodiesel.

Willie: We call it BioWillie Biodiesel.

Bill: BioWillie Biodiesel.

Willie: I started to call it Willie Bio, but that's Roger's. I ripped him off enough already.

Bill: I see him smilin' down on us right now.

Willie: Yeah, right.

Bill: You mentioned something that caught my attention. You said organic food, and you're right, I don't know of any truck stops that are into a study on what truckers should eat for health.

Willie: Well, I think a lot of truckers know what they like to eat, but it's difficult to find it everywhere. I thought maybe if there was a brand-new biodiesel truck stop along with organic food, it might attract somebody.

Bill: Some big things happening, and we are going to open up the lines here in a minute. Willie Nelson's new product—BioWillie

Biodiesel—is going to be a big thing. It cuts down on the smoke and the atmospheric problems. It's leaves cleaner air. Am I reading that right?

Willie: Yeah, much cleaner, like 80 percent cleaner, I think.

Bill: What else do we need? I mean, it's going run the vehicles, make the air cleaner, it's going to be a new product that's not going to be hard to find. It's going to be everywhere. We'll keep you abreast of all that.

Willie: And it's going to help the farmers. You know, we've been losing 300 to 500 farmers a week. I went to Washington a few weeks ago with a Democrat and a Republican. We went there with Dennis Kucinich from Ohio, who introduced this bill that would help the farmer stay on the land and let him grow fuel for us and for everybody.

Bill: Man, man, man. I love it. I love it.

Willie: So if you know a congressman … I met seventy congressmen up there and gave them all literature, wrote them a letter, so ya'll should call everybody that you know and say, Hey, check that out.

Cindy: Do you know what the bill is, the bill number?

Willie: I could find out for you. Dennis Kucinich will know. I'll find out.

Bill: Let's jump to JoJoLady real quick. JoJoLady, where you calling from?

JoJoLady: I'm driving down the highway just outside of Big Springs, Texas.

Bill: You got a bad signal on ya. Go ahead, talk to Willie.

JoJo: Hi, Willie.

Willie: Hello. How you doin'?

JoJo: Real good. So glad to talk to you.

Willie: Thank you.

JoJo: I'll make it quick, in case we get disconnected. I wanna find out about the fuel and how long before it's going to be everywhere we can get it.

[...]

Willie: It's just a matter of spreading the word at all the truck stops. When they begin to realize that this is the future, that one of their pumps will be biodiesel, and you'll have a chance and a choice when you go in there. Who knows how long that will take. I think it's sooner than we thought. I think all this new talk and publicity will help bring it about. I'm talking to some people from Love's truck stops, and they're very interested. The more folks like that are interested, the quicker that it will happen.

Bill: Here is what I want you to do now. This is very important. When you have something you can add, truck stop locations or anything, I want you to call me or have someone call me and let us spread the news, because this is not something that is idle. It is very important. It is a product that is going to help so many. I don't want to be repetitious, but keep me informed on what we can do to help out. ... Don Neering. I gotta put Don [on]. Don, talk to Willie. We don't have much time, but my pal, Don, talk to Willie.

Don: Hey, Willie. I want you to keep on doing what you're doing, bud. Let's get it available everywhere.

Willie: Well, help me put out the word. Tell everybody about it, and you're right, the more of this we can get around, the better. I think school buses should start burning it, all the trains should start, all the diesel engines should start using it. In fact, I think that the government should insist on it. Because it helps so many people.

Don: Well, I know that it's a good product from everything I have been able to research on it, and with your name behind it, I hope that just takes off and flies away, man. This is exactly what our industry needs, and I'm sure proud you're behind it.

Willie: Thank you very much.

Bill: Don Neering, one of the best. Thank you, Don, and appreciate you, pal. I have about a minute and a half. This has been a rapid hour here. First off, thank you for the time. You've always been there for me. I can't thank you enough. Just for the fact that you are Willie Nelson.

August 31, 2005

Bill: Hello, everybody. I didn't know that the mic was open. Welcome back into our most humble program. Glad to have you with us today, wherever you are. Of course, it's Wednesday, and that means it's trash day at our house. Gotta put that trash out.

Cindy: It's lawn day and it's trash day.

Bill: Also, it happens to be a Willie Wednesday ... Willie Nelson.

Willie: Where do I put the trash?

Cindy: Better hurry, Willie.

Willie: How ya doin'?

Cindy: Fine, how are you?

Willie: I'm good, Cindy. Where's old Bill today?

Cindy: Right there ... right here.

Bill: I'm right here.

[...]

Let's go to the phones. We got a long list. We got a bunch. They love you, pal, these people love you. Hi to JoJoLady. JoJoLady, talk to Willie.

JoJoLady: Hi, Willie. How ya doin'?

[...]

Willie: Okay. What can I do for you today?

JoJo: I wanted to ask a few questions. We're on our third tank of biodiesel, and our truck is running real smooth. We're getting better fuel mileage. It's really kinda a surprise. We've got a great big old cat engine in our truck, and it's doing real good on the biodiesel. But we're having a problem finding it at truck stops.

Willie: Well, yeah, and that's going to continue to be until all of us figure out a way to get the plants built and the government to help us. In the meantime, though, we have a problem out here. We find it when we can, and when we can't, we burn what we have to burn.

JoJo: Yeah. Yeah, we were in Illinois … we got an 11 percent blend. In Amarillo, we found a 20 percent blend. And that ran real good. The biggest problem is that it's in gas stations but not in the places where the trucks can get to.

Willie: I was talking to Carl today, and we were talking about the blends that he got down there. He's got a B95. He may be out of that now, but that's one of the blends. He has the B20 … there's a 60/40 blend. Hopefully a lot more places will carry all these blends.

JoJo: Yeah We're just hoping that there will be some more out there real soon. What can we do to help move that along? Who do we talk to?

Willie: Well, anybody and everybody. Yesterday I was in Duluth, Minnesota, and they called it Biodiesel Day. The mayor was there, some young guys around there brought in 500 gallons of biodiesel for our buses and trucks to fill up. The press was there and made a big deal out of it. So I think more and more things like that need to happen to get more and more people talking about it. Kind of demanding that we get some help out there for the people that want to grow it and the people that want to buy it and sell it. We just need some help.

Bill: JoJoLady, thank you very much. We have to move to the next one here. We have a new place out there now.

Cindy: I announced it earlier that in Virginia off of I-81 exit 273 at the Liberty Truck Stop they have the B20 blend.

Bill: B20. Alright, that's a good blend.

Cindy: Liberty Truck Stop. Virginia. I-81 exit 273.

Bill: And now, Willie, I guess you have heard and that I mention that there are truck stops—the Flying J's truck stops out there in Nashville, Tennessee, area—are out of fuel. This makes biodiesel much more of a necessity. We've got to have it.

[...]

Cindy: I need to do something real quick here. I received an e-mail from CoCoPuff earlier this morning saying that Grumpy was going to be in Grand Forks, North Dakota, by one o'clock today. Wanting to know where might be a place to buy biodiesel up there. So I just went on to biodiesel.org. And you look across the top, there's a link there that says Find Biodiesel. Click on that, and a little drop box comes down and you can pull up the retail fueling sites. Okay. In North Dakota there's one in Devil's Lake, North Dakota. That's the Farmers Union Oil Company at 600 Highway 2, West Devil's Lake, North Dakota. They have all blends there. Then we have the Farmland Co-op at 617 Main Avenue, that's in Oakes, North Dakota, and they have all blends there as well. I hope that helps you out, Grumpy.

[...]

Bill: Okay now, pal, there is so much interest in biodiesel. I was watching the events happening with Hurricane Katrina on TV last night. One person did say we have to have alternative fuel. And you said something a moment ago, the government is goin' to have to get involved so the people can manufacture it.

Willie: We have got to have more plants, and we gotta have more incentives for farmers to grow various crops that can be used for fuel. All of the other alternative energies—wind, water, solar—our government must step in and do something for us now. Charity begins at home. It's time to take care of our own right now.

Bill: On a show several months ago, when you first told me about the biodiesel, I thought, This sounds interesting. But I had no idea, and I don't think you did either at that time, the situation we would eventually get into as we are facing today, a major hurricane in the Gulf ... where it's not something that would just help out, it's something we've got to have.

Willie: Yeah, and I had no way to know that any of these horrible things were going to happen. Every disaster that we have in any way affect us, and the energy cost, and all the things that we've been concerned about are happening to us now.

Bill: That's right, pal, that's right. And, again, this will put the farmers back to work. By the way, when is the Farm Aid show? I was going to ask you, that's coming up next month, I know.

Willie: September 18, in Chicago at Tweeter Land, I think. Tweeterville … Tweeter Field … Tweeter Center?

Bill: Alright, we are going to take a break here.

Willie: Tweeter … Tweeter Field.

Bill: It's always fun with you here on Wednesdays.

Willie: Thank you. Same here.

Bill: I've had people say they wish you were here five days a week. Doing the entire show.

Willie: That would be too much manure.

Bill: We'll let Willie take a break, we'll take a break. Don't forget all phone calls. Subject: Willie Nelson. Still got a half hour to go with Willie.

[…]

It's Willie Wednesday with country music Hall of Famer Willie Nelson. You're on *Open Road* 171. We'll be right back.

[**Commercial break**]

Bill: Okay, welcome back in to our Willie Wednesday. Texas governor Rick Perry says he expects evacuees to start arriving within the next twenty-four hours at the Houston Astrodome. He says Louisiana governor Kathleen Blanco asked him this morning if the Astrodome could house the 23,000 people currently being sheltered at the Superdome in Louisiana, and he quickly agreed. He says that even before the request, Texas officials had been talking about using the Astrodome as a long-term shelter for people already stranded in Texas because of the storm, but in case you folks have not heard, Houston is going to be moving the people from the Superdome to the Astrodome. Those folks stuck in the massive horrible thing out there in Louisiana … New Orleans. Let's go back to our good pal Willie, my boy, my boy.

Willie: Hey, Bill.

Bill: We've never seen anything like this, and of course, just picking up on what has been said so many times during the past couple of days, we talk about the fuel issue, the truck stops running out of fuel. We already don't have enough fuel to meet the demand. But we have to get to more when there's something tragic: the loss of human life.

[…]

Incidentally, I had the occasion to be with Peter Bell and several more at the Biodiesel Breakfast at The Truck Show. Some very good people there. And I saw more interest than I have ever seen on the subject of Willie Biodiesel. I think a lot of good was done there pointing in the right direction. We are trying to get you to manufacture enough. Look at this. I'm getting an e-mail coming in now. Everybody's wanting it. And you hear the people talk about it. They get more miles per gallon. All that has to be done is it has to be manufactured. Time to say that it's got to be done. Let's go to NoHandle.

Willie: NoHandle?

NoHandle: Yes, sir.

Willie: How you doin' today?

NoHandle: Hell, I'm ridin' around through North Carolina into Virginia right now.

Willie: Well, that's gotta be pretty nice.

NoHandle: Well, it's nice and pleasant, getting a little cool because of all of the cloud cover. And the moisture of that little hurricane. But it's alright.

Willie: Yeah, well, I wish you all the luck up there. What can I do for you today?

NoHandle: Were you aware that there's a flood of peanuts on the market?

Willie: Well, I knew that there was a relaxing of the allotment thing on peanuts. And I heard that there were a lot of people going around the leasing of the peanut ground. I did hear that.

NoHandle: Well, there was a major flood in the market. They've overproduced peanuts this year, and since the peanut crop is so large, the government has bought up all of the excess peanut allotment and they are going to just take the peanuts off the market. In order to hold the price up, which means the government is holding peanuts.

Willie: I didn't know that.

NoHandle: Yeah, which means nothing is going to be done with them. They're either going to be stored or thrown away.

Willie: Well, that doesn't sound right.

NoHandle: Shit yeah, it don't sound right, if you can make bio-diesel out of it! It's just supposed to keep the price of actual peanuts that go for peanut butter and everything else. They've already calculated the amount that it would take, and they are going to take the rest off of the market.

Willie: Well, you know, the original diesel engine was designed to run on peanut oil.

NoHandle: Yeah, well, you might get ahold of Mr. Bill. He might contact somebody in the agricultural department and find out where the peanuts are and what they are going to do with the excess peanuts.

Willie: I think Jimmy Carter would know, and so, if any of his folks are listening, maybe they can give us a call and let us know what is going on in the peanut world. 'Cause he knows all about that down there in Georgia.

Bill: We'll check on that. That's a good fuse you just lit there too.

'Cause all the peanuts could certainly be used. Don't throw them away, don't put them in a warehouse. Put them to work making biodiesel. Thank you so much, pal. LoneWolf is next.

Willie: LoneWolf, how are you today?

LoneWolf: Hey, what's happening?

Willie: Everything's great. Where are you?

Lone: I just left town, heading toward Alabama.

Willie: Alright.

Lone: Yes, a couple of weeks ago, you were on Bill's program and you were talking about these little small biodiesel plants that you could get for pretty reasonable.

Willie: Right.

Lone: Yeah. Do you have any information on where and how I can get any information on how I can get one of those things?

Willie: As a matter of fact, I was just looking at those. There is a little one, a $2,900 biodiesel plant that would make 40 gallons every two days. I found it on the Internet. I think I found it off of the biodiesel.org or one of the other biodiesel sites. But I think if you go to Google and punch in "biodiesel plants," et cetera, you might find it.

[…]

This one I think operates on vegetable oil.

Lone: Yeah, that's what I was looking for. I live down in East Texas.

Willie: Yeah, go Google biodiesel [and] you can find out about them.

Lone: Yeah, well, my wife did a lot of research on biodiesel here recently, or a couple of weeks ago, and she checked on the biodiesel plants. [Laughing] Like $40 million!

Bill: Thank you, thank you, brother, we appreciate it. Getting those plants and everything everywhere. We just looked a while ago … more biodiesel out in the Midwest and out in California, of course, but looking where there are areas it is available, but we have to make it available everywhere. And it can be done. Get those peanuts out of storage and get them to work.

[…]

Rich, you there?

Rich: Yeah, I'm a truck driver up here in Wisconsin, and I sing local. And we really need this biodiesel, and I can't get ahold of it in central Wisconsin here, and I don't know if it's the government keeping it out but … it seems like it's all over down there.

Willie: Well, yeah, we have run into some guys in Wisconsin, and, in fact, we are in La Crosse now, and last night we had some folks come to where we were in Duluth, Minnesota, last night—Duluth, right? Duluth—and brought us some biodiesel, and they are very much aware of biodiesel, and, you know, they have been aware for a long time.

Rich: Yeah, we sure do need it. We need guys like you out there promoting it. You are doing a lot for it [nationally] and locally, and you're doing a lot for country music, and I appreciate the show I had the other night. You are a class act.

Willie: Thank you very much, and nice talking to ya.

Bill: Rich, the one thing is, spread the word. Spread the word when you hear us talking about it here. Get on the horn and spread the word, and it is available, 'cause it is available. Not only available, it is being used successfully. Let's go to Michelle. Michelle, are you there?

Michelle: Hello.

Willie: Hello, Michelle, how are you?

Michelle: Oh, just fine, Willie. My husband and I are both huge fans. Personally, I would like to thank you for all your help you have given to the American farmers with your Farm Aid concerts. Someday I would like to get to Luckenbach, Texas. My husband said to tell you, if you ever get to Gatlinburg, Tennessee, he will cook you the best Texas-style steak you have ever had in your life.

Willie: Well, I will look forward to that. Thank you.

Michelle: And could you someday maybe write a song about us lady truckers?

Willie: Write a song about lady truckers?

Michelle: You betcha.

Willie: Alright ... Mother Truckers.

Michelle: Sure.

Willie: Bill, don't get your mind in the wrong place here. This is serious.

Bill: No, I'm just thinking that has a nice ring to it.

Willie: Yes, it does, and that's a good idea ... someone should do it. Mother Truckers of America, we're proud of you!

Bill: You bet we are. Michelle, we are proud of you, angel. Thank you.

[...]

Catfish, are you there?

Catfish: Yeah, I'm here.

Willie: Hey, Catfish, it's Willie. How are you doin'?

Catfish: We're good. Y'all?

Willie: Oh, everything's alright. Where are you?

Catfish: Cartersville, Georgia, is the last sign I've seen on I-75.

Willie: Alright. How's the weather around there?

Catfish: Sun shining, very few clouds.

Willie: Well, that's good.

Catfish: Can I mention a TV show and a host that's on that show?

Bill: Yeah.

Willie: Sure, go ahead.

Catfish: On Spike TV there is a show that's called *Trucks*, and, uh, there's a guy that hosts it named either David Stacy or Stacy David. The name is hard to remember because it's the right name but hard to remember. Anyway, this last Sunday he had on there a biodiesel, what do you call it, refiner?

Willie: Yeah.

Catfish: He took thirty-five gallons of cooking oil he got from the restaurant for free, and, you know, he used the cooking oil and put it in the drum there, and he done the test that you have to do to see what needs to be added. And, you know, I thought that was real cool, for him to do that like that.

Willie: Yeah, it is, and, you know, we were talking about the little biodiesel plants that you can get now that you can make your own biodiesel. If you happen to have a restaurant, it might be worth it, or anybody that has any kind of vegetable oil.

Catfish: That's true. What I thought was neat about it, he started off with thirty-five gallons and run it through the process. You know, you have to do a little chemical analysis and stuff like that, Red Devil wine and ethanol, I think. Racing gasoline. Even though he filtered the sludge, he still wound up with twenty gallons of usable diesel fuel. Everything else on the show talked about how good it was and where to get it and all that. I just wanted to give a shout-out to him. It's a good show.

Bill: Thank you, Catfish.

Willie: Well, thank you. On a larger scale, that's what they are doing for us in Maui, and my car is run on biodiesel made from the same thing: vegetable oil gathered from various restaurants around the island. It is an up-and-coming idea, and lots of people are thinking about it.

Bill: Thank you, pal. Thank you very much, Catfish.

[...]

Willie, I can't thank you enough for being here. Our Willie Wednesday is becoming more important every single week, and everything you do makes us even more safer, and I can't thank you enough for taking the time.

August 6, 2006

Bill Mack: Alright, ladies and gentleman. It's Wednesday, which means it's time for the one, the only, Willie Nelson. I just hope I've got him here. Are you there, pal?

Willie: Yeah. Can you hear me, Bill?

Bill: Ah boy, you are coming in like Del Rio, Texas.

Willie: Alright. How you doin', Cindy? How y'all today?

Cindy: Doin' great, Willie, how are you? Good to hear you.

Willie: You too, darlin'. What are you up to, Mr. Mack?

Bill: Wait, did you call me 'darlin''?

Willie: Sweetheart. Baby.

Bill: Hey, listen … boy, you've been busy, busy, busy. So good to talk with you, my friend, my friend.

Willie: You too. You gave me some good information the other day. Sort of food for thought. Did you remember what you told me about the emissions and everything that is going to be reduced because of all of the biodiesel that was used last year?

Bill: Yeah, did you get a copy of that?

Willie: I don't have a copy of that in front of me, but I did get a copy, and I thought that was real interesting stuff there.

Bill: We'll bring that up after a while. After the break I will look that up. Lots of things are happening. Here, one says they are building … I got this from Larry Shannon. Larry does the *Overdrive Trucking News*. It says, "They are going to build a biodiesel plant in Rock Port, Missouri, about twelve miles from my place. … will use soybeans to make it. Thirty million gallons a year is what they expect to produce. Lots of farmers out here are getting ready for action."

Willie: Well, that's great. There's quite a few of those plants coming along. There's one in Gonzales, Texas. That just opened up; they have the BioWillie there. I think Triple T Truck Stop, or restaurant, whatever … service station. It's a new one. I wanted to give them a plug.

Bill: Honest to God. Here's one … this is from Shannon, Larry Shannon again, and he says he drove over to Nebraska City yesterday. Stopped at the Staff Brothers Station, and they are really selling biodiesel there. He says, "I don't know if it's

Willie's brand, but they got it." That's the talk. This guy does the *Overdrive Trucking News*. He's an old pro, and also works with Jim Wright, speaker of the House. And he says everybody is speaking of biodiesel.

Willie: That's great. I was just reading some stuff here about Austin: "Austin opens nineteen B20 pumps"—that's biodiesel pumps. "A city known for its live music is now renowned as the nation's newest biodiesel enthusiast. Nineteen Shell stations in the Austin, Texas, area have pumps that carry a blend of 20 percent biodiesel and 80 percent diesel."

Bill: Here's the thing, with diesel jumping up three cents a gallon more since Monday, it's just something that has to be done. I'm proud of what you are doing. Where are you located today?

Willie: Today I am in Connecticut. On the day after tomorrow, I go up to the Boston area. But I have a day off today, and I'm hanging out.

Bill: Talking to Willie Nelson. It's a Willie Wednesday, ladies and gentlemen.

[…]

You know, here's that thing, Willie. It says, "[In 2005], BP fuels contained more than 575 million gallons of biofuels [in the United States], eliminating about 1 million tons of carbon monoxide. … Today, they're available in more than twenty states." It's a start. BP, meaning Beyond Petroleum, and that's where we gotta go.

Willie: Yeah, and that's in this country, right?

Bill: That's right.

Willie: If you think about it globally, and all of the biodiesel that is being used and the ethanol last year, then that's making a pretty good dent in it for one year.

Bill: I tell ya, it is. Here's something else now… have you heard about the Orient taking notice of biodiesel? Obviously, you have. China, all of a sudden, is using more fuel, which is certainly holding up the process a bit in this country, with prices and things. Now we are getting the fumes. They did a study on a mountaintop in California, and we are getting the heavy load of problems in the air from China. And now there's a word out China [has] picked up on the thoughts toward biodiesel. I think all countries—except the Middle East, they don't have to worry about it—but I think a lot of countries that have to have importing done on diesel fuel, fuel in general, I think they are going to say, Hey, if we can grow it, let's get it done.

Willie: You know, on a smaller scale, over in the Hawaiian Islands, over there we have to import all of our gasoline and oil and diesel. So at this moment, I think biodiesel on the Islands is like $1 cheaper than regular diesel and gasoline.

Bill: I believe you are right.

Willie: How much money you can save if you don't have to ship it in. You know, if you can grow it.

Bill: Here's a note from Barry Cohen. I don't know whether I sent this to you or not. "Dear Bill, We are involved with building a $55-million biodiesel plant, and I want to get ahold of Willie. Willie doesn't do the building of these things, but certainly he can pass messages on to other people who handle those."

Willie: Well, and, you know, these phone calls probably help a lot too. There's a lot of people out there who are interested in investing in biodiesel and ethanol, and they just really don't know how to do it. But with more people calling in saying, Hey, this is happening over here and that's happening over there, then maybe people can start thinking about How can I jump in there and do something and accomplish something. And also, you know, they may make a couple of bucks in the end, you know.

Bill: Absolutely, and you can e-mail us if you want, if you have any questions, and we will forward questions or statements … would love to get your statements about biodiesel.

Cindy: Yes, just e-mail us at billmack@billmackcountry.com.

Bill: Simple as that.

[…]

[**Commercial break**]

Bill: Hello, walls. Ladies and gentleman, it's a Willie Wednesday. We have the man with us again. I'm so happy.

Willie: Hey.

Bill: Did you enjoy your break?

Willie: Oh, I took a little nap, went for a jog, a swim, did a few push-ups, and here I am.

Bill: Willie Nelson, ladies and gentleman, and so glad to have Willie with us. Dr. Bruce Kemp, retired … I don't know what. I guess he is retired from being a doctor. But he says, looking at Willie Nelson's biodiesel enterprise, that you have been helping him keep that foot of his in the door of a mighty big industry for American homegrown biodiesel. "Got me to thinking about something out here in Southern California. I was curious to know if you or Willie have ever heard about a seven-year-old San Diego–based company that's been producing and selling its product to all four branches of the military, national security, several foreign governments, and other multibillion-dollar companies here in the States. Have you heard of Ethos?"

Willie: No, I haven't, but I have always known or heard that the military was into biodiesel a long time and have been using it in tanks and things over here and overseas. Why they didn't open it up to us is obvious, but I understand they have been using it a long time.

Bill: He says, "I know everybody just rolls their eyes and kisses them off as another fuel additive, but I beg to differ. Here's a few examples of what we are talking about: Allied Waste Management, an $8 billion company, second largest in the

United States, started using EthosFR with biodiesel in their trash trucks stationed in south San Diego County, in a town called Chula Vista."

Willie: That's great.

Bill: They have been doing this for six or seven years. They have received awards for doing a bang-up job for reducing particulate matter that is smog and stuff in Chula Vista. About 500 tons in a single year. This is from Dr. Bruce Kemp, that ... oh, okay. With the global warming and other things happening, it's something that has to be done. We have got to get this biodiesel put into action.

Willie: Yes. My wife, Annie, has written me a note here. It says that it is more about reducing particulates in the air than even gas availabilities. That's true too.

Bill: You know, Chrysler has come out with a new SUV that uses B5, or something like that.

Willie: There is just more and more. You read about John Deere, you read about these folks with biodiesel already in the equipment, already in the tractors. This is just happening more and more around the country, around the world, really. It's sort of ... necessity is the mother of invention, and as we really started to need an alternative energy, somebody went in and figured out where it was.

Bill: Now the question is, the biggest question we are getting—I know you are getting the same question—Why isn't more being done by those who can get it done? In various leading outlets, in the nation's capital and other government spots. Let's go to the phone.

[...]

Lou's on the line. Hello, Lou, how are you?

Willie: Hello, Lou.

Bill: Wait, just a minute. I think I've got Lou.

[...]

Lou: I've got a couple of questions, plus I have for you, got a statement from my son.

Willie: Alright.

Lou: James Slydel, out there, he drives for Lewis Trucking. He says your biodiesel is the best fuel he has ever bought. Looking to see if we can get some up here in Tennessee.

Willie: Well, that's wonderful. Tell him thank you. I think there are some plants up there in Tennessee. I don't know the specifics on it, but hopefully we will have you some biodiesel before long.

Lou: That's good. Now for the questions. When you going to get into biogasoline to help the poor man like us?

Willie: Well, I'm getting into the ethanol end of it and out promoting plants out around the country. So I am very much aware of the need for ethanol and [to] help people who drive regular cars. More and more ethanol plants are being built and more and more places where you can find it. But it's kinda like biodiesel; it's going to take a while for it to get around and get people to figure out what to do about it and make some money, et cetera. But it is going to happen.

Lou: That's about the size of it, Willie.

[...]

Bill: Thank you, my friend.

Willie: It's nice of you to call. And call us back here again sometime. ... I found out why them guys who herd all them sheep wear a big old robe.

Bill: Yeah?

Willie: Because them sheep can hear a zipper from a mile away.

Bill: Alright, ladies and gentleman. As always, it's been fun. Next week?

Willie: For sure.

[...]

Bill: That is it. The one, the only, Willie Nelson. Stay on the line

here, keep your calls coming in. We're just taking a little break.
171 *Open Road.*

Fuel for Thought

My knowledge of biodiesel is still very much a work in progress. Every day I learn of new ways to make it. And every day
I ask myself, Why can't we grow here what can be grown
abroad? It will take all the biofuels from everywhere to
satisfy our demand on this planet. In order to protect our
local producers, it's important to produce at least 50 percent
of our biofuels locally. Ideally, producers in Hill County,
Texas, for example, would grow their cotton and soybeans
locally for a profit, and any surplus would be exported.

An ideal world would use no fossil fuels. It is possible
to run the world on biofuels and alternative energy such
as hydrogen, solar, wind, and so forth. Countries such
as Brazil are showing us the way. Several states are using
biodiesel blends in all diesel sold and are also mandating
blends of ethanol in all gasoline. New biodiesel plants are
cropping up all over the country. This is a great start; let's
all keep going. Let's put America's family farmer back in
business: the business of growing our fuel.

I'm looking around and I see they're taking my soap-
box away and I have to wrap this up. When I first found
out biodiesel really works, I saw a light at the end of the
tunnel for family farmers. I had just about given up on
finding the solution that could save the American family
farmer, but at the next Farm Aid press conference, all I
could talk about was biodiesel. All I wanted to talk about
was biodiesel, because I believe that there is an answer,
there was an answer, and this is the answer. Today the oil
companies and the farmers have the opportunity to work
together. No matter what side of the oil rig you're on, both

sides can successfully stay in business if the United States turns to biodiesel for its enormous diesel needs. Everyone can come out a winner, especially the consumer.

We started Farm Aid to try to help save the American family farmer, but now it looks as though the family farmer may save America.

Please consider biodiesel for all your diesel needs. You'll be glad you did.

I'm Willie Nelson and I approve this message.

Afterword

The Future of Alternative Energy

> My interest is in the future because I am going to spend the
> rest of my life there.
>
> —Charles F. Kettering

When I was asked to write a piece on the future of alternative energy, my first reaction was to debate the use of the world *alternative*. The thing is, there isn't really an alternative, so the use of the word in "alternative energy" is somewhat a misnomer.

Neither fossil fuels nor nuclear energy present a sustainable long-term energy strategy for the world; both rely on finite resources, whether this be fossilized plants or animals, or uranium (and eventually, when that runs out, thorium). Furthermore, the toxic wastes they produce are slowly choking our planet and producing irreversible changes to our world that future generations will have to live with the consequences of.

By comparison, the "alternative," based on a future of sensible energy reduction and efficiency measures and power generated from renewable resources, will not be to the detriment of future generations, and unless the Sun stops shining, the energy will be there in abundance forevermore.

Yellow dwarf stars, like our Sun, live for around 10 billion years. Our Sun is already about 5 billion years old. With the exception of tidal energy, which relies on the gravitational pull of the Moon on the Earth (and the Moon isn't going anywhere soon), all renewable technologies rely in some way on solar-driven processes. That means that we needn't worry about the security of renewable energy for about another 5 billion years. That should be enough time to work something else out.

In order to look forward to a bright future, we need to look back and learn from our mistakes. In *Fates Worse Than Death*, Kurt Vonnegut said, "What other fates worse than death could I name? Life without petroleum?" As we are heading rapidly toward a "life without petroleum," this raises some interesting questions. We are heading toward a Malthusian catastrophe at breakneck speed. The Western world is a slave to oil and, as such, a slave to those countries that produce that oil. The only way for countries to free themselves from this tyranny is by taking energy production back into their own hands.

Evidence of this is becoming more obvious by the day, despite the best attempts of a small group of commercial and political interests that try to maintain the status quo. Unfortunately, the strength of the fossil fuels and nuclear lobby is embedded within the institutions that rule and govern us, and its influence reaches to the higher echelons of power.

Despite this fact, the tide is slowly turning in favor of renewable-energy technologies, and as the cost of obtaining oil—both in dollars and human lives—mounts, people will begin to wise up to the alternatives.

The only way that we will move to an alternative-energy future is by the collective effort of the populace to save energy and transition to sustainable technologies. We are already seeing evidence of this change: renewable energy, once the reserve of those considered eccentric, is now positioned firmly in the mainstream.

John M. Richardson Jr. said, "When it comes to the future, there are three kinds of people: those who let it happen, those who make it happen, and those who wonder what happened." Be one of the ones who make it happen. Reading this book is the first step. The next step you take is up to you. But remember, your effort, however small in the scale of things, is helping to bring the future forward.

The Future of Energy

Solar

To ensure the continued survival of the human race, we need to look for solutions to our energy needs—beyond petroleum. This fact is so clear that British Petroleum has been using "Beyond Petroleum" as their slogan—notice that the big boys are sitting up and listening. Denis Waitley said that "losers live in the past. Winners learn from the past and enjoy working in the present toward the future." The oil companies are slowly realizing that their days are numbered. So much does BP realize that they need to evolve or die, they are now one of the biggest producers of solar panels in the world. Smart companies like BP recognize that the solar-energy market is growing by 30 percent per year* and that if they are going to survive as energy providers in the twenty-first century, they need to be participants in that market.

One of the big challenges of materials science has been to reduce the amount of exotic materials that are required in the technologies that will deliver a sustainable-energy future.

* http://www.bp.com/sectiongenericarticle.do?categoryId=3050463&contentId=3060093

Sass Peress, CEO of ICP Solar, said that "the solar industry is the poor relation of the microchip industry," commenting on the fact that solar manufacturers tend to get silicon that is not up to standard for manufacturing microchips.

One technology that shows great promise is that of "printable components." The technology used in your home ink-jet printer is being used by companies to produce components for sustainable-energy systems by depositing exotic materials onto a membrane just as if they were ink. This has great potential to reduce the costs of solar cells and the membranes used in fuel cells.

One such company is Nanosolar. Two of its most famous investors are Sergey Brin and Larry Page, founders of Google. The company is developing technologies that will enable it to be able to "print" solar cells using a small amount of exotic material to produce what is termed a "thin-film" solar cell on a cheap plastic substrate. This technology is *very* cheap and cost effective, with the downside of being lower efficiency than other types of solar cell. However, the advantages are many: the flexible plastic sheet has the potential, if produced in scale, to be used to cover large surfaces such as a building cladding. The benefit is thus derived from the ability to cover large areas with low-efficiency solar cells at relatively low cost.

Solar cells that are integrated into building cladding and roofing systems have shown great promise. Their success lies in the fact that not only are they generating clean renewable energy, but they are also replacing an item of building fabric—saving the cost of that item.

By moving from what is effectively a small-batch production process used to produce traditional solar cells to a large continuous process that can readily be scaled up, the cost of solar cells could fall through the floor.

Nanosolar has just secured the funding to build a factory that will be able to print 430 megawatts of solar panels per year; with its ability to mass produce cheap solar cells, this factory will dwarf all of those that are currently operating.

Other solar technologies also show interesting promise. At the moment, the solar cells we see in common use are based upon photovoltaic technology; however, in 1991, discoveries were made by Michael Gräetzel in the field of photoelectrochemical solar cells. Rather than relying on expensive silicon, these cells rely on a different technology that can be likened to the process of photosynthesis that plants use. The benefits are that this is a cheap technology that can be produced on a large scale when the technology is perfected. At present, cells have been demonstrated with conversion efficiencies of around 10 percent; however, this is expected to rise to around 33 percent in the future.*

Of course, we can already harness solar energy using the photosynthesis process that plants use by producing biofuels. This book extols the virtues of biofuels at great length; however, what can we expect to see in the future?

Hybrids and Biofuels

A world powered solely on biofuels is unrealistic. Even assuming a drastic reduction in our energy consumption, there is not enough productive land to meet all of our energy needs from biofuels. However, as a transitional technology, biofuels show amazing promise due to the fact that they can be moved easily using our present infrastructure for moving fossil fuels. As the price of petrol and diesel increases, biofuels will gain wider acceptance and be available more widely.

---

* Brian O'Regan and Michael Gräetzel, *Nature* 353, no. 24 (October 24, 1991): 737–740.

Already, many of the major auto manufacturers are offering "hybrid vehicles." The benefits to both manufacturers and consumers are clear: manufacturers are able to prolong the life of a technology that they are familiar with (the internal combustion engine) while developing new alternatives and consumers are offered greater efficiency than standard internal combustion engines while more-advanced technologies are being developed.

I do not believe that hybrid vehicles are anything more than a short-lived fad in the interim period while cheap fuel-cell technologies are developed.* Neither can I see the kudos in buying a large hybrid vehicle when a small conventional vehicle would meet your needs (and, in some cases, have better fuel consumption). People need to change their mind-set from competing with the next-door neighbor to having technology that is appropriate for their needs.

However, a general increase in energy prices will encourage other sustainable technologies. It is my belief that after the present generation of vehicles with internal combustion engines, we will begin to see fuel-cell vehicles permeate the market, and for some applications, battery vehicles may enjoy limited success.†

---

* In my opinion, hybrids are a very good way to begin the transition away from the internal combustion engine and a way to highlight that goal. The technology that has been and is being developed will help us build better electric motors, build more advanced and more efficient transmissions, as well serve as an incentive to design advanced battery technologies, all of which are crucial to our evolution away from internal combustion engines.

† Again, I think that the transition to a fuel-cell style of transportation will take very long, probably more than twenty years, and encounter many obstacles. One of them is the fact that we do not have enough of the material that it takes to build as many fuel cells as we would need to replace the internal combustion engine. Until they figure out a better way to do this, we are in a tough spot. One of the best ways for us to reduce our energy dependence, both foreign and local, is to pay a lot more attention to recycling

Many technologies that have come to shape the world were at first dismissed on economic grounds or as having little practical relevance. Few could see uses for the lightbulb or electricity when first proposed. It is easy to look back in retrospect and laugh at such apparent short-sightedness; however, in doing so, we must ensure that we do not sneer at newly proposed technologies that may eventually come to be a part of everyday life.

Wind

Solar is not the only renewable technology in which rapid progress is being made. The cost of generating electricity from the wind has fallen dramatically since the industry's birth in the early 1970s. The average wind farm pays back the energy used in production in the first three to five months after installation.*

While the costs of oil and gas have steadily risen, the costs of renewable energies are steadily falling. We are fast approaching the point where these lines will cross and producing power from fossil fuels will be more expensive than from renewable energies.

One of the reasons for the fall in costs is the economies of scale granted by the engineering technology that allows us to build larger turbines than ever before. One prediction suggests that in ten years' time, we could see wind turbines

---

and reusing by taking older vehicles that have worn out, and replacing their engines and other components, and upgrading them with more-efficient technologies that we have in place today. It takes far less energy to repower a twenty-year-old Honda by putting in a new engine, shocks, tires, brakes, steering components, and updated electronics than it does to build a new one. The savings are dramatic and can be realized today.

---

* Milborrow, David, "Dispelling the Myths of Energy Payback Time," *Wind Stats* 11, no. 2 (Spring 1998).

that generate 20 MW.[†]

There will always be those who object to the aesthetics of wind generators; however, though many people do not find them objectionable, new wind turbines are in development that are visually more attractive and less obtrusive than conventional wind generators.

Strides are already being made in the right direction. The Aerogenerator, designed by a collaboration of Grimshaw architects (who devised the large biomes that are a landmark of the Eden Project, Cornwall, UK) and Windpower Ltd., is unlike any wind turbine you have ever seen. Designed for offshore use, the turbine can produce up to 9 MW in windy conditions. Unlike traditional wind turbines, which rotate around a horizontal axis, the Aerogenerator is comprised of two arms that spin around a vertical axis, like a record deck.

The Dutch government commissioned a study to look at alternatives to regular wind farms that would produce power while appearing less intrusive in the flat Dutch landscape. One of the proposals was for "wind-trees," an organic art form where up to eight turbines would be anchored to a central trunk, providing an installation that was visually interesting as well as generating clean "green" energy.

Overcoming public opinion is a major task that needs to be accomplished. Many are still opposed to wind turbines, which they see as ugly blots upon the landscape. The mentality of "not in my backyard" needs to be overcome in favor of a notion of collective responsibility for our energy production.

Again, technology is leading the way in seeking solutions to make wind turbines more attractive in more

[†] Andersen, P., "Om 15 år har vi møller på mere end 20 MW." [In 15 years we will have turbines of more than 20 MW]. *Eltra* magasinet, November 10, 2001.

environments. It strikes me as patently odd that many are opposed to the erection of wind turbines yet seem to take little offense at the huge amount of advertising that we are bombarded with from every direction: billboards and sale signs on every street corner.

Innovative British consultancy XCO2 has developed a solution that capitalizes upon this mentality: wind turbines that incorporate an array of light-emitting diodes controlled by an embedded processor within the turbine. The diodes are illuminated in sequence to draw a picture in the sky as the turbine spins. The power for the display is provided by the turbine, which produces a surplus of power that can be used elsewhere. As the turbine blades spin at high speed, the lights are illuminated in turn to produce full-color pictures seemingly hovering in the air. This provides two income streams for the turbine: the clean, sustainable power produced and the advertising revenue generated by selling the display space.

Doing some crystal ball gazing, I see no reason why we will not see these urban turbines in evidence in the streets adjoining Times Square, New York, or Piccadilly Circus, London, within the next couple of decades. Their bright lights are attractive and enticing and make wind energy interesting for all.

Hydroelectricity
Hydroelectric technologies are already used at a large number of sites worldwide; however, large hydroelectric sites have the disadvantage of potentially being incredibly disruptive to local ecosystems. The proportion of electricity generated from large hydro schemes may increase modestly over the coming years; however, the number of economically exploitable large sites is finite, and, as such,

I think that we are unlikely to see a massive increase in large-scale hydropower.

Small-scale microhydropower, however, shows promise, as there are a large number of streams and rivers from which power can be extracted with negligible damage to the local ecosystems. Unobtrusive river generators can be used on a local level to meet some energy needs.

One area where I feel hydroelectric power shows great promise is in pumped storage.

The energy produced from renewable sources, though intermittent, in many cases is predictable. We know in general that sometimes the sun is shining and sometimes it isn't, sometimes the wind is blowing and sometimes it isn't, so we can safely assume that over a period of time, this will balance out—the average amount of energy produced over a period of time can be predicted with some reliability.

The challenge, therefore, becomes matching instantaneous supply to instantaneous demand. This requires some form of storage technology. At the moment, for such large amounts of energy, batteries and fuel cells do not present an option, other than on a very local level. However, pumped storage may offer some solutions.

It is my belief that in the years to come, we will see an expansion in pumped storage in which water is pumped from a low reservoir to a high one using "spare" energy then allowed to flow back down to the low reservoir through a hydroelectric generator when energy is required. On a local and regional level, this technology has the potential to even out the discrepancies between supply and demand.

Wave and tidal power is another area of renewable energy that has hitherto received relatively little attention. Wave generators that are moored offshore, though they may receive some objection from shipping, are relatively unobtrusive and, as such, provoke little objection from members of the general public. Although this area is still in its infancy, I believe that it will undergo significant expansion in the future.

Where sustainable energy-generating devices can fulfill more than one function, they will find success in the future. Where wave and tidal power generation can be incorporated into a wider schema of coastal protection and flood defense, they will find great favor.

We have seen how climate change is causing irreversible changes to our weather patterns. Moreover, we have witnessed the vulnerability of cities to the elements in the tragic scenes that were witnessed in New Orleans following Hurricane Katrina.

James Lovelock asserts that the damage we have done to the planet and our climate is irreversible and that we will now have to plan carefully in the years ahead to protect what we have built.

Many global cities, notably London and New York, are vulnerable to rising sea levels. Both will require engineering on an unprecedented scale if they are to be protected from the irreversible damage of a growing ocean. It is unlikely that governments worldwide will stand back and surrender their great cities to the sea. Extraordinary engineering will be employed to protect these assets from our own self-imposed destruction, and by the time these great schemes are implemented, they will include a significant element of renewable generation technology.

Already, a replacement Thames barrage has been mooted to protect the city of London from rising sea levels, and even at this early stage of discussion, the inclusion of renewable technologies has been suggested.

Another interesting experimental process that has

the potential to generate sustainable power in the future through water is that of reverse electrodialysis, also known in some circles as blue energy. This phenomenon exploits the difference in salt concentration between river water and seawater. Using some very expensive plastic known as an ion-specific membrane, it is possible to separate positive ions from negative ions and thus generate clean renewable energy. Blue energy stations could be located where river deltas meet the sea, with the only waste from the process being brackish water that can readily be disposed of into the sea. This technology still requires significant development. At the moment, the cost of the membranes is a real barrier to innovation, as is biofouling, in which biological matter from the water used to feed the process clogs the membrane. However, expect to hear more about this process in the years to come.

Considering Supply and Demand

Successful mass implementation of renewable technologies requires carefully matching supply to demand. Though we can pursue a strategy of trying to meet all possible demands with an excess of supply, it would also be prudent to examine strategies of matching instantaneous supply to demand.

We are living in an increasingly connected society. The Internet and networks prevail and reach into our everyday lives. It is a small wonder that the advanced data-transfer techniques afforded by the Internet are not being employed to manage our energy demands in a more dynamic and responsive manner. We already see laptops that operate at maximum speed while main supply is available then operate at maximum efficiency while running on battery. We see appliances with "economy" modes as awareness of energy efficiency spreads. Now imagine relinquishing just a little bit of that control back to the grid. Imagine the grid controlling your electrical devices, reducing their power consumption at times when electricity is scarce. This is known as transient demand-side management.

Transient demand-side management will mean a more dynamic, responsive grid in which the power available is linked to the price of energy, which is also linked to control of demand. Rather than paying a fixed fee to your utility company, imagine a scenario in which the energy your house produces was bought and sold on a spot market depending on the demand for energy. Similarly, the price you pay to buy energy back from the system depends on the energy available and the demand that is out there from other consumers. Such a system allows users of energy to make informed choices about when they are going to use energy. By optimizing their routines, it is possible to save money.

In a report calling for upgrades to the grid and energy distribution system in the United States, Patrick Mazza said that "today's grid is mostly composed of traditional technologies. Thomas Edison would recognize most of it." If the world is to meet the new challenges that large-scale microgeneration brings with it, then the grid of tomorrow will be virtually unrecognizable from the grid of today. Already, a number of high-profile power failures have highlighted the vulnerability of our present systems after years of drastic underinvestment in infrastructure. The need for change has already been highlighted.

César Chávez said that "once social change begins, it cannot be reversed. You cannot uneducate the person who has learned to read. You cannot humiliate the person who feels pride. You cannot oppress the people who are not afraid anymore. We have seen the future, and the future is ours." By empowering citizens with the ability to produce their own energy, they become stakeholders in the process of energy production and use rather than mere consumers of energy. Rather than just being purchasers of a product, they become engaged with the process of producing that energy and, as a result, become liberated from the tyranny of centralized power production.

When looking at the evolution of energy production and distribution systems, we can see how they have evolved over time from small, centralized hierarchical arrangements in which a single company supplied a few local consumers to more complex national grids in which a number of companies producing energy are connected to a greater degree on national and regional levels. The adoption of renewable-energy technologies is only going to add to the complexity of these networks: the shift from centralized production to decentralized local production will result in greater connectivity at a local level. Ultimately this is leading us to closer integration and networking on a local level, whether those networks be physical networks, cabling, and infrastructure for the distribution of energy or social networks such as cooperatives and local renewable initiatives.

It is my belief that the adoption of renewable-energy technologies as a major global producer of energy will lead to a fairer and more equitable society. Centralized control of energy will subside to a renewable future where the production of energy is distributed and owned by society. Society benefits as a whole from the production of energy, and as people become participants in the process of producing that energy, they begin to respect it as a resource and use it sensibly and conservatively. This creates a feedback loop that reaffirms the need for responsible production of energy and conscientious use of energy that is not present in the current linear structure in which energy is produced by a utility and consumed by a consumer.

Final Thoughts on the Future

Whereas the late twentieth century was seen as the information age, a time when the world went through a process of rapid interconnection, networking, and connection allowing the free flow of information between individuals, so the age we are entering will forever be remembered in the annals of history as the energy age. We are entering an era of the white heat of sustainable technology. Whereas the 1960s brought us a blend of cutting-edge innovation such as the Concorde and quirkier innovations such as the hovercraft, so the twenty-first century will bring a range of energy-producing innovations, some practical, some verging on the esoteric. However, at this early stage, it is important that all technologies be developed to their fullest potential, as the chasm between the energy we produce sustainably and the energy we *need* to produce sustainably is a very wide one.

At this early stage in the game, when we are barely scraping the surface of the innovations that will lead our world to becoming totally sustainable, we need to remain open minded and not discount any solutions. We can only begin to thin out the solutions when we are approaching the end of the road on our journey to sustainability.

We saw how the information age brought with it increased freedom through the free flow and exchange of ideas and knowledge. We have seen the transformative effect that the Internet has had on countries where the control of information resides with centralized powers that eke out the information they see as necessary to achieve their aims to the populace. And we have seen how those powers have resisted the ability of the masses to exchange information freely.

So will the energy age bring with it increased freedom from the free flow of energy? The role of the consumer will change subtly from consumer to consumer-producer. The process of trading energy will be more of a balance across the system than a stream of production and consumption. This will have a transformative effect on the way our governments perceive the security of our nations. In the manner that "man's security comes from within himself," so too will nations will begin to feel secure as their energy needs are met from within.

Rather than energy being eked out by OPEC to the rest of the world at a rate that befits their own ends, nations will have the ability to produce energy cleanly at a rate that befits their own economies and needs. In an analogous manner to the way tyrannical powers try to control the free flow of information, so the powers controlling our present sources of energy will resist; however, it is my firm belief that self-determination will prevail.

I look forward to our entry into the era of the "white heat of sustainable technology."

—Gavin David James Harper

Helpful Resources

Biodiesel America

www.BiodieselAmerica.org

Web site created by Josh Tickell, early proponent of biodiesel, with variety of resources, including the story of the Veggie Van

Biodiesel Magazine

www.bbibiofuels.com/biodieselmagazine

Monthly magazine dedicated to the biodiesel industry

BioDiesel Now

www.biodieselnow.com

Web site with variety of biodiesel resources, including local and regional contact information

Biodiesel Solutions

www.biodieselsolutions.com

Provides information on personal biodiesel processing

BioWillie

www.biowillieusa.com

The name says it all!

Farm Aid

www.farmaid.org

A nonprofit organization whose mission is to keep family farmers on their land and to restore family farm–centered agriculture

Iowa State University Biodiesel Program

www3.me.iastate.edu/biodiesel

Offers a biodiesel workshop

National Biodiesel Board

3337a Emerald Lane, P.O. Box 104898

Jefferson City, MO 65110-4898

www.biodiesel.org

National trade association representing the biodiesel industry as the coordinating body for research and development in the United States

National Renewable Energy Laboratory (NREL)

www.nrel.gov

The nation's primary laboratory for renewable energy and energy efficiency research and development

Piedmont Biofuels

www.biofuels.coop

Located in North Carolina, a regional leader in biofuel production

University of Idaho Biodiesel Fuel Education Program

www.uidaho.edu/bioenergy

Involved in biodiesel research since 1979

environmental benefits statement

Fulcrum Books saved the following resources by using
100% post-consumer waste paper for this book

Trees	42
Energy	29 Million BTUs
Greenhouse Gases	3,649 pounds
Water	15,147 gallons
Solid Waste	1,945 pounds

Calculations based on the research by Environmental
Defence and the Paper Task Force.

Manufactured by Friesens

Reg shelf

HQ